New Land, New Language

Maxine Berger and Martha Seigel
LaGuardia Community College

New Readers Press

Sources
p. 65 Lower East Side Tenement Museum Encyclopedia, Table 3, "Expenditures of a Working Family in
New York City, 1874," p. 71; http://tenement.org/encyclopedia.pdf (viewed June 8, 2006).
p. 68 Lily Merman, "Growing up on the Lower East Side," unpublished memoir, collection of the LESTM.
p. 103 Sevcenko, Liz, ed. From Immigrant To Immigrant; A Guide for New Arrivals In New York. Lower East Side
Tenement Museum, 1999.

Other information and stories have been drawn from the following:
"Tenement Times," a bulletin published by the Lower East Side Tenement Museum from 1989 to 2002.
"Around the Kitchen Table," a video developed to accompany "The Immigrant Connection," on which
New Land, New Language was based.

New Land, New Language
ISBN 978-1-56420-524-7

Copyright © 2007 New Readers Press
New Readers Press
Division of ProLiteracy Worldwide
1320 Jamesville Avenue, Syracuse, New York 13210
www.newreaderspress.com

Printed in the United States of America
9 8 7 6 5 4 3 2 1

All proceeds from the sale of New Readers Press materials
support literacy programs in the United States and worldwide.

Acquisitions Editor: Paula L. Schlusberg
Design & Production Manager: Andrea Woodbury
Illustrations: Lower East Side Tenement Museum, Linda Tiff
Production Specialist: Carolyn Boehmer
Cover Design: Carolyn Boehmer

Contents

To the Teacher

New York City has always served as a mecca for new immigrants from all over the world. The tenement apartment building at 97 Orchard Street started out as the home for hundreds of these newcomers. Throughout the years, many immigrants have left, but more have taken their places. All these people are connected by their common experiences as *new* Americans.

New Land, New Language uses the immigrant experience as a common unifying theme and draws upon it to teach communication skills. The theme is reinforced and brought to life by stories that feature immigrants from the past and the present. The purpose of the book is not only to teach students practical words and language skills, but also to show students that immigrants throughout the 20th century struggled with the same kind of problems and challenges that often seem to overwhelm immigrants today.

As ESL teachers who have worked extensively with many immigrants of various backgrounds and language levels, we believe that this book will connect all students, regardless of their background. We have found that students are interested in learning about other immigrants' lives, as well as fulfilling their own immediate needs. The lessons in this book help students do both.

Each lesson has a specific theme relating to everyday life. The lesson begins with the definition of a **Keyword** that highlights a specific facet of the immigrant experience. Students are then introduced to a **Reading** about an immigrant's life in early New York City. The teacher is encouraged to lead a **Discussion** tying together the keyword and the reading.

Following each reading are questions **About the Story**. Students should first answer these on their own before sharing their answers with the class. These comprehension questions

check students' understanding of the content. **What's Your Experience?** asks questions that are meant to stimulate a dialogue (or raise further questions) among the students about the themes in the reading as those themes relate to students' own lives and times. Questions in **What Do You Think?** ask students to interact with the story and/or the characters. They might be asked to delve into a character's motives, give advice to a character, predict a character's thoughts or actions, or make inferences about a character's personality. Any of these questions can be answered orally or in writing at the teacher's discretion.

While this book is not intended to be a comprehensive grammar book, each lesson includes grammar and vocabulary exercises that relate to the lesson's theme. **Words You Can Use** presents and offers practice in new vocabulary that students can use in everyday life. **How You Say It** presents basic grammar points that are used in everyday communication. These are then practiced in exercises that also relate to the theme of the lesson. **Put It Together** gives students a chance to practice using the new vocabulary from Words You Can Use in combination with the grammar point from How You Say It.

Every lesson has a second **Reading** selection. In many cases, this reading contains one or more authentic stories from immigrants who lived on New York City's Lower East Side. It may also include additional factual material. This second reading selection is shorter than the first reading, but continues to focus on the same theme. Following the reading, students are asked **What Does It Mean?** First, they guess the meanings of selected words in **bold** by using context as an aid to comprehension. Then, students can look up the words in a dictionary. We feel that reading will improve if students are encouraged to actively guess meanings rather than just to depend on a dictionary. Teachers can expand on these vocabulary exercises by having students write their own sentences using the new words and/or by having students repeat the same activity with unfamiliar words not in bold. Finally, there is a prompt to stimulate a **Discussion**.

In **Picture It**, a graphic organizer helps students organize their ideas from the lesson by putting them into a visual format such as a graph, a time line, an idea map, or a ladder. After completing a graphic organizer, students will better be able to visualize how their ideas relate to each other. **Apply What You've Learned** takes students from the book to real life. Here students work on activities using the lesson themes to produce materials that are relevant to their own lives.

Each chapter concludes with **Write About You**. On this journal page, students are asked to write about their own experiences related to something in the lesson. These writings can be shared with the teacher and classmates if desired. The teacher may also respond to the writing by giving students positive feedback. In addition, the journals can be used as springboards for discussions in which students ask questions and comment on each others' written ideas.

We have designed the lessons so that teachers can expand upon any one section through additional discussion, grammar practice, or writing activities, depending on the class composition, goals, and frequency of meetings. Through these materials, we aim to give teachers flexibility and to give students new tools and insights that will help them cope with the challenges and joys of living in the U.S., just as immigrants before them have always done.

Acknowledgments

We would like to thank Ruth Abram and Steve Long of New York City's Lower East Side Tenement Museum for initiating the concept of using immigrants' stories to help newcomers to the U.S. learn English. This book would not have had an authentic voice without the wealth of rich stories and photos from the museum's archives. Some of the stories in *New Land, New Language* are based on articles in "Tenement Times," an in-depth bulletin published by the Lower East Side Tenement Museum from 1989 to 2002, containing articles about 97 Orchard Street, the Lower East Side, and the immigrant experience. We are grateful to all the immigrants who shared their personal experiences. We also want to express our appreciation to the BIL Trust which funded this project early on. We are especially indebted to Barbara Lovenheim for her endless hours of editing and designing the original book and for overseeing the project in its early stages. Also a note of thanks to Hesper Desloovere for helping to pull out the immigrants stories from the multitude of interviews, transcripts, oral histories, and other resources in the Tenement Museum. Finally, it has been our pleasure working with our editors at New Readers Press, Terrie Lipke and Paula Schlusberg, who helped transform this project into a book accessible to so many new Americans.

Martha Siegel
Maxine Berger

LESSON 1

Coming to America

Nostalgia is the feeling that you miss something from your past. Do you ever feel **nostalgic** or homesick for your native country? What do you miss most about life there?

A postcard showing Kastoria, Greece, the hometown of the Confinos, a Jewish family who lived in 97 Orchard Street
(collection of the Lower East Side Tenement Museum)

In the 1800s and 1900s, many immigrants came to New York City from around the world. Some immigrants left behind beautiful homes in their native countries. In New York City, they moved into crowded tenement buildings. Tenements were old apartment buildings for poor families. This story is about the Confino family, who came to New York City from Greece almost 100 years ago.

Abraham and Rachel Confino with four of their five children, around 1913
(collection of the Lower East Side Tenement Museum)

Abraham and Rachel Confino and their five young children lived in the Greek town of Kastoria in the early 1900s. They lived in a large and beautiful house. They had a lot of land with gardens and fruit trees. There were vineyards and a lake nearby. Then their huge house burned down in a fire. The Confinos lost everything. They decided to make a new start in the U.S. In 1913 the family moved to New York City. They lived at 97 Orchard Street. This was a five-story tenement building on the city's Lower East Side. Many immigrants lived there.

The seven Confinos crowded into a three-room apartment. It was on the fourth floor of an old, dark building. There was only one window in the front room. There was no heat or hot water. There was also no bathtub or shower. When the Confinos wanted to wash, they had to heat water on the stove. They bathed in the sink. The toilet was in the hall. Other families shared it. Most family members had to sleep on mats on the floor. Abraham's youngest child, Little Jacob, slept in an orange crate. At night, rats ran around the apartment and scared him.

One hundred years ago, life was very difficult for these poor, unskilled immigrants. Abraham and his family had trouble getting jobs since they couldn't talk to factory owners and shopkeepers in English. Many immigrants set up their own clothing factories. Here they employed their friends and relatives who spoke the same language. Abraham first got a job as a peddler. Soon he opened his own apron and dress factory. The Confinos had many problems, but they were able to start a new life in the U.S.

About the Story

1. The Confinos left a beautiful large home in the countryside and came to a tenement building in New York City. Describe the home they left behind.

2. Describe the Confinos' living conditions. How was life unhealthy in these tenement apartments?

3. How did immigrants who lived in the tenements keep themselves clean?

4. Describe how the Confinos lived in their apartment.

5. Many Immigrants from the same country worked together. Why do you think this was so?

What's Your Experience?

Life was very difficult for immigrants 100 years ago. Do you think they were sorry they came to the U.S.? What about you? Is your life difficult here? How do you feel about your decision to come to the U.S.?

What Do You Think?

1. The Confinos missed many things about their life in Greece. What advice would you give them to help them adjust to their new home in the U.S.?

2. How do you think the Confinos' living conditions affected their family life?

3. Abraham worked with people who spoke the same language as he did. Do you think it's a good idea for people with the same background to live and work together? Why or why not?

Words You Can Use: Sequence Words

Sequence words, or time order words, make the order of events or actions clear when you read, speak, or write. You can say *first*, *second*, *third*, etc., to show when something happened. You can also use other words to do this. Some of these words are: *before*, *after*, *next*, *then*, *finally*, and *last*.

Example: In the English alphabet, here are the first five letters: *A B C D E.*
- *A* comes *first*.
- *Next* comes *B*, which is *after A* and *before C*.
- *Then* comes *D*.
- *Finally*, *E* is the *last* letter of the five.

Try It Out

Write eight things you did yesterday. Put them in order of when you did them. Then, on a separate sheet of paper, write a paragraph about your day yesterday. Use as many sequence words as you can.

_____

_____

_____

_____

_____

_____

_____

How You Say It: Contractions

The verb *to be* is often shortened. You use an apostrophe (') in place of the missing letters.

Affirmative	**Negative**
I am = I'm	I am not = I'm not
We are = We're	We are not = We aren't/We're not
You are = You're	You are not = You aren't/You're not
He is = He's	He is not = He isn't/He's not
She is = She's	She is not = She isn't/She's not
It is = It's	It is not = It isn't/It's not
They are = They're	They are not = They aren't/They're not

Try It Out

Rewrite the sentences. Use contractions. Use two forms if possible.

Example: I am Korean. = I'm Korean.

They are not here. = They aren't here./They're not here.

1. He is from Mexico. _____

2. You are in this class. _____

3. It is not the capital of Ecuador. _____

   _____

4. You are not a citizen. _____

5. They are immigrants. _____

6. She is not good at English. _____

   _____

7. I am good at English. _____

8. We are Americans. _____

9. We are not Americans. _____

   _____

10. It is a beautiful country. _____

Put It Together

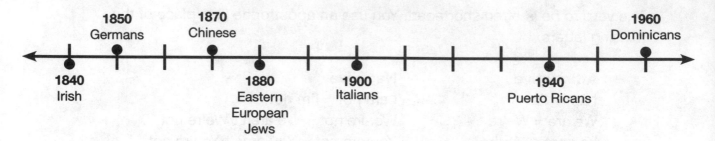

1850
Germans

1870
Chinese

1960
Dominicans

1840
Irish

1880
Eastern
European
Jews

1900
Italians

1940
Puerto Ricans

A. Look at the time line. It shows when different groups of immigrants started coming to New York City's Lower East Side. Answer these questions. Use a sequence word.

1. Which group came to the U.S. first?
2. Which group came here next?
3. Which groups came before the Chinese?
4. Which groups came after the Italians?
5. Which group came here last?

B. Write sentences about your classmates' nationalities. First write the name of the person. Then make statements using affirmative and negative contractions.

Examples: Jorge and Maria: They're Dominican. They're not Chinese.
Jin: She's Chinese. She's not Russian.

Name	Affirmative	Negative

Ernesto Ibanez came to the U.S. from El Salvador. He was nostalgic for his homeland. This is a story about how he felt when he came here.

Some of the words in the reading are in bold. Try to guess the meanings of these new words. Then find the meanings in a dictionary.

Arriving in the U.S.

It is very hard for people to change their lives when they come to a new country. Ernesto had to change not only his life, but also his **expectations** about the U.S. When he came to the U.S., he got the surprise of his life. New York City looked like it did in postcards. But the postcards didn't show how people really lived. He saw many people **suffer** here. He was very sad to see what his mother's life was like in New York City. Ernesto's bedroom in El Salvador was bigger than his mother's whole apartment.

Ernesto also felt sad because he lost something very important in his **journey** to the U.S. He felt he would never again be the same person he was in his native country. Ernesto lost his **identity**. He said that this was something that no one notices—only you. He was **depressed** for several weeks. He missed his native country and his life there, but he had to think about his future in the U.S.

What Does It Mean?

New Word	Your Guess	Dictionary Definition
expectations	_____	_____
suffer	_____	_____
journey	_____	_____
identity	_____	_____
depressed	_____	_____

Discuss

Ernesto's postcards showed what New York City's buildings looked like. But they did not show how people really lived. What were your expectations before you came here? How are things different from what you thought they would be?

Picture It

Write the year of your birth on the bottom step of the ladder. On each step, write an important year in your life. On the line to the right, write about the important event that happened in that year. Make sure you put all the years and events in time order.

Then, report to the class about your life. Use sequence words.

```
20____
  TODAY    _____
           _____

           _____
           _____

           _____
           _____

           _____
           _____

           _____
           _____

           _____
           _____

20____
           _____
19____
YEAR OF BIRTH   I was born in _____
```

Apply What You've Learned

You are an immigrant to this country. People will want to find out information about you, and you will want to find out about other people.

Interview a classmate you do not know very well. Ask questions to get the information on the form below. Write notes about the person's answers. Fill out the form below with the information about this person. Then, introduce your partner to the class.

Name: _____

Nationality: _____

Language: _____

How long in the U.S.: _____

Family: _____

_____

Job in native country: _____

Job in the U.S.: _____

Interesting fact about the person: _____

_____

_____

Write About You

Ernesto Ibanez recorded his memories in a journal. In this book, you will write down <u>your</u> memories, thoughts, and feelings.

How did you feel in the first few months after you came to the U.S.? Were you excited, happy, afraid, depressed? Describe what happened to you and your feelings about being here. Do you still feel that way, or have your feelings changed?

_____

_____

_____

_____

_____

_____

_____

_____

_____

_____

_____

_____

_____

_____

_____

_____

_____

_____

LESSON 2

Making a New Home

A **home** is more than just a building where you live. It's the place where you feel you belong. What was your home like in your native country? How would you describe your home now?

The kitchen of the Rogarshevsky apartment at 97 Orchard Street, recreated by the Lower East Side Tenement Museum
(collection of the Lower East Side Tenement Museum)

In 1901, Abraham and Fannie Rogarshevsky arrived by boat at Ellis Island. They came from Lithuania with their children. The family moved into 97 Orchard Street. Here is their story.

Abraham and Fannie Rogarshevsky came to the U.S. with their six children. There were four boys and two girls. They moved into 97 Orchard Street, where Fannie's parents already lived. At that time, over 100 immigrants lived in the building. Most of the immigrants were from Russia and Poland. Others were from Germany, Ireland, and Italy.

The Rogarshevskys lived in three tiny rooms. The apartment was 325 square feet. The four boys slept in the front room. They all slept together on a couch and stretched their legs onto chairs next to the couch. The two girls slept in the kitchen on a small bed that folded up. Abraham and Fannie slept in a bed in the tiny back bedroom. During the hot summer, the family often slept on the fire escape or up on the roof. Many other tenants also slept outside to keep cool.

At first there was no electricity. Gas lanterns lighted the apartments. There was no hot water, so Fannie had to boil water on the stove for washing and cooking. Each floor had only one indoor toilet in the hallway. Two families had to share the toilet. In 1916, the building finally got electricity.

Fannie and two of her sons lived in the building until 1941. When they finally moved out, the building was in very bad condition. In 1988 this building was turned into The Tenement Museum. Many apartments were recreated to look like they did in the 19th and early 20th centuries. In this way, visitors can see how the Rogarshevskys and other immigrants lived when they first arrived in this country.

Members of the Rogarshevsky family in front of 97 Orchard Street, around 1915
(collection of the Lower East Side Tenement Museum)

About the Story

1. When the Rogarshevskys moved to 97 Orchard Street, there were very few modern things. What didn't they have that most families have today?

2. What did the family do to live without these modern things?

3. Describe how the Rogarshevsky family slept in their small apartment.

4. When Fannie and her sons left the building, it was in very poor condition. Why do you think this happened?

5. Today, 97 Orchard Street is a museum. What did the museum do to show us how immigrants once lived there?

What's Your Experience?

The tenement apartments at 97 Orchard Street are now part of a museum. Many other apartments like them no longer exist. Have you ever gone back to a place where you used to live? What is it like now? Is it the same as you remembered it to be?

What Do You Think?

1. How do you think small apartments like the ones at 97 Orchard Street affected family life and relations with neighbors? How do you think the family members were able to have some privacy?

2. Families in the early 1900s had very few modern things like we have today. How do you think your family would get along in an apartment like the Rogarshevsky's?

3. The Tenement Museum shows us how some immigrants lived 100 years ago. Why do you think it's important or interesting to know about this?

Words You Can Use: In a Home

There are many different things you can find in each room of a house or apartment. Here is a kitchen, living room, and bedroom. Label the items that you know from the words below. Compare answers with a partner.

Air conditioner
Bed
Bookshelf
Ceiling
Chair
Computer
Couch
Cupboard
Curtains
Desk
Dishes
Door
Dresser
Floor
Lamp
Microwave
Mirror
Nightstand
Picture
Pillow
Refrigerator
Rug
Sink
Stove
Table
Telephone
Television
Wall
Wastebasket
Window

How You Say It: *There is* and *There are*

The phrases *there is* and *there are* come at the beginning of sentences. They show that something exists or tell where something is.

Examples: *There is—There is* a table in the kitchen. *(There's* a table in the kitchen.)

There are—There are dishes in the sink. *(There're* dishes in the sink.)

We often use *there is* and *there are* in the negative. When we do this, we usually use the contractions *there isn't* or *there aren't*.

Example: *There isn't* an air conditioner in the kitchen.

There aren't any books in the bedroom.

To ask a Yes/No question, put *is* or *are* first.

Example: *Is there* a computer in your living room?

Is there any milk in the refrigerator?

Are there any beds in your kitchen?

In negative sentences and questions, use *any* with plural nouns or noncount nouns (that is, nouns that cannot be used in a plural form).

Try It Out

Find out about your partner's home. Ask questions using *Is there?* or *Are there?*
Answer your partner's questions using *There is, There isn't, There are,* or *There aren't.*

Describe your partner's home to the class.

Example: *Are there* any flowers in your home?

No, *there aren't.*

Question:_____

Answer:_____

Question:_____

Answer:_____

Question:_____

Answer:_____

Question:_____

Answer:_____

Put It Together

Write five differences between the Rogarshevsky apartment and the house or apartment you live in now. Use *there is, there isn't, there are,* and *there aren't.* Use complete sentences. Include some vocabulary words from **How to Say It**.

Share your ideas with the class.

Rogarshevsky Apartment	My Home
There isn't a TV in the Rogarshevsky's apartment.	There is a TV in my home.

The building at 97 Orchard Street was like many other apartment buildings where immigrants in New York City lived. Here is a description of the apartments that they called home.

Some of the words in the reading are in bold. Try to guess the meanings of these new words. Then find the meanings in a dictionary.

97 Orchard Street

The tenement building at 97 Orchard Street was built in 1863. It housed 20 three-room apartments. Only the front room received direct light, and that was often **blocked out** by other tenement buildings. **Residents** could not tell if it was nighttime or daytime. The bedroom did not have any fresh air or daylight. There was no toilet, no shower, and no bath. In the early days, toilets were located in the backyard and **shared** by everyone. Every apartment had a sink, but no **plumbing**. Early residents got water from a hand pump in the backyard and carried heavy pails up to their apartments. Some immigrants had to walk up five stories on un-lighted staircases. It probably took several trips just to fill the sink.

Apartments were very cold, and there was no hot water. Mothers washed their children with a sponge and cold water each morning. Once a week, they gave the children a warm bath in the kitchen sink. A small amount of hot water came from a heater **attached** to the stove. Families washed themselves and their clothes in the kitchen sink. They even prepared food there.

What Does It Mean?

New Word	Your Guess	Dictionary Definition
blocked out	_____	_____
residents	_____	_____
share	_____	_____
plumbing	_____	_____
attach	_____	_____

Discuss

How are apartments or homes different today than they were at 97 Orchard Street 100 years ago? Do you think any people in other parts of the world still live like that? Explain.

Picture It

Imagine that you can live in your perfect house. What would you put inside? Draw pictures of what you want in your home. Label each item. If you don't know a word, ask your teacher or a classmate.

Share your drawing with the class. Describe your dream house.

Bathroom	Bedroom

Living Room	Kitchen

Apply What You've Learned

Write a list of problems with your apartment or home. Tell a classmate about each problem. Ask what you can do to make things better.

Problems	Solutions
My apartment is too dark.	Buy a new lamp.

Write About You

Write about a home that you remember well. Describe the home. What was special about it to you?

_____

_____

_____

_____

_____

_____

_____

_____

_____

_____

_____

_____

_____

_____

_____

_____

_____

_____

_____

_____

_____

LESSON 3

Getting Around the Neighborhood

An **ethnic neighborhood** is an area where many people from the same country live. In New York City, for example, there are areas where many Greek, Hispanic, or Chinese families live. Where do you live? What kind of neighborhood is it? What ethnic groups live in your neighborhood?

The front entrance of a tenement,
around 1908
(collection of the Library of Congress)

Adolfo and Rosaria Baldizzi came from Sicily, which is part of Italy, to live in New York City. Here is the story of their experience with the neighborhoods they lived in.

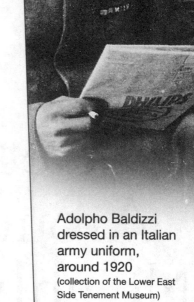

Adolpho Baldizzi dressed in an Italian army uniform, around 1920
(collection of the Lower East Side Tenement Museum)

The Baldizzis made their first home in the U.S. in a Sicilian neighborhood on New York City's Lower East Side. Their daughter, Josephine, was born there in 1926, and her brother, John, was born a year later.

Rosaria was very unhappy when she first moved to New York City. She missed the trees from back home. She also hated the dirt and the small apartments. The streets were noisy and crowded with horses and people. Many of the people sold goods on the street. Only later, Rosaria began to love New York and the U.S.

Soon the family moved nearby to 97 Orchard Street. That was when Josephine was two years old. For seven years, the family lived in a tenement with other immigrants. Josephine and John went to public schools. They also went to an Italian school to learn to speak Italian.

Adolfo knew the neighborhood well. He often walked around the streets to look for work. Sometimes, he took his children to the public baths. Here they washed themselves and met friends. The family also went sightseeing. They went to Sara Roosevelt Park on the East River. They traveled by subway to Coney Island. They even went to see the Statue of Liberty once. Rosaria often went to church, the movies, and the Italian theater.

Josephine felt very safe playing near the house. Family and friends were always close by. John was braver than Josephine. He explored the neighborhood by himself. He also played baseball, and he boxed. John always came home late for dinner.

Everything the Baldizzis needed was right there in their neighborhood.

About the Story

1. How did Rosaria feel when she first came to the U.S.? What made her feel this way?

2. The Baldizzi children went to a public school and an Italian school. Why did the parents send them to two schools?

3. Why did people go to public baths on the Lower East Side?

4. Where did the Baldizzi family go when they had free time?

5. Why was 97 Orchard Street a good place for the Baldizzis to live?

What's Your Experience?

The Baldizzis lived in a poor and crowded neighborhood. However, they were able to enjoy many things there. What are some good things about your neighborhood? What are the things you don't like? Do you think most of your neighbors agree with you?

What Do You Think?

1. The Baldizzis moved to an Italian neighborhood when they came to the U.S. Why do you think they chose to live with other Italians?

2. The Baldizzis liked to go sightseeing when they first came to the U.S. What places would you tell them to visit today?

3. Josephine liked to stay close to home. Her brother went to see different neighborhoods by himself. What can you tell about their personalities?

Words You Can Use: Words that Give Directions

When you move to a new place, it's easy to get lost. You often have to ask someone for directions. Here is a list of words that can help you find your way.

Have you ever used these words to give directions? Discuss their meaning with the class.

Turn left	Turn right	Go straight
On the left	On the right	On the corner
Highway	Intersection	Cross street
Stop sign	Traffic light	Across the street

Go straight for _____ blocks/miles.
Go one block (two blocks/three blocks).
Go north (south/east/west).
Continue until you come to _____ .
Take the train/subway/bus.

Try It Out

A. Write directions for how to get to your home from school or work.

_____

_____

_____

_____

_____

B. Write directions for how to get from your home to your best friend's house.

_____

_____

_____

_____

_____

_____

How You Say It: Prepositions of Location

A **preposition** is a word that can be used to show a direction or where something is. Some prepositions are: *between, next to, on, at, near, behind,* and *across from.*

Examples: There is a subway station *on* my street.

The Tenement Museum is located *at* 97 Orchard Street.

Orchard Street is *between* Ludlow Street and Allen Street.

There is a bus stop *near* the museum.

The post office is *across from* the bank.

The public library is *next to* a park.

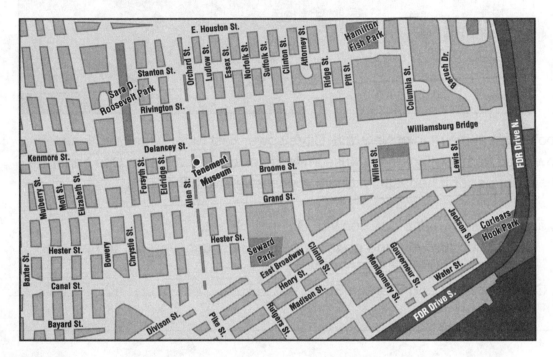

Try It Out

Look at the map of New York City's Lower East Side. Answer each question orally using the preposition in parentheses.

Example: Where is Rivington Street? (*between*)

Rivington Street is between Stanton and Delancey Streets.

1. Where is Allen Street? (*near*)

2. Where is Sara D. Roosevelt Park? (*between*)

3. Where is Corlears Hook Park? (*next to*)

4. Where is the Tenement Museum? (*on*)

Put It Together

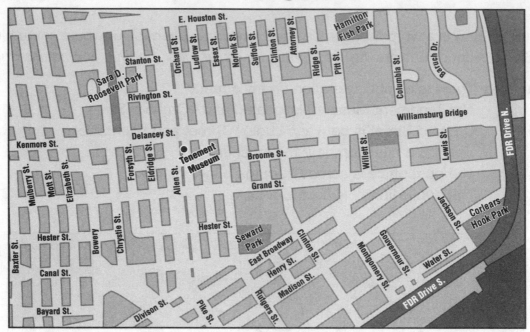

Look again at the map of New York City's Lower East Side. Write directions telling how to go from the Tenement Museum to the places listed below. Use separate sheets of paper if necessary. Share your answers with the class.

Example: Walk *a half block north* to Delancy Street.
Then *turn left* and go *three blocks west* until you get to Forsyth.

1. Corner of Allen and Stanton Street _____

_____

2. Corner of Hester and Chrystie Street _____

_____

3. Intersection of Eldridge and Canal Street _____

_____

4. Seward Park _____

_____

5. Attorney Street _____

_____

Classified Ads

Classified ads in newspapers have to use shortened words. Look at this ad for an apartment. Use the list of common abbreviations to understand the ad.

Some of the words below are in **bold**. Try to guess the meanings of these new words. Then find the meanings in a dictionary.

Apt to rent Furn 2 BR, 2 Bth, EIK, LR, all new Appl, A/C throughout. Elev bldg, Avail June 1, $1000/mo +util., Orchard Brokerage 212-555-1212.

BR = bedroom	Util = **utilities**
Bth = bath	WU = walk up
EIK = eat-in kitchen	Avail = **available**
LR = living room	Reno = **renovated**
Appl = **appliances**	A/C = air conditioning
Elev = elevator	Cond = condition
Mo = month	Bldg = building
Incl = included	Furn = **furnished**

What Does It Mean?

New Word	Your Guess	Dictionary Definition
furnished	_____	_____
appliances	_____	_____
utilities	_____	_____
renovated	_____	_____
available	_____	_____

Discuss
What things are most important to you when you want to buy or rent a new home?

Picture It

Here is a map of a neighborhood. Pretend this is where you live. You have many things to do on your day off:

1. buy groceries
2. mail a letter
3. get money
4. meet a friend at the park
5. go to the movies

Identify where your home is. Draw it on the map. Starting at your home, draw on the map the route you will take to do at least three of these things. Tell a partner how to get to each place.

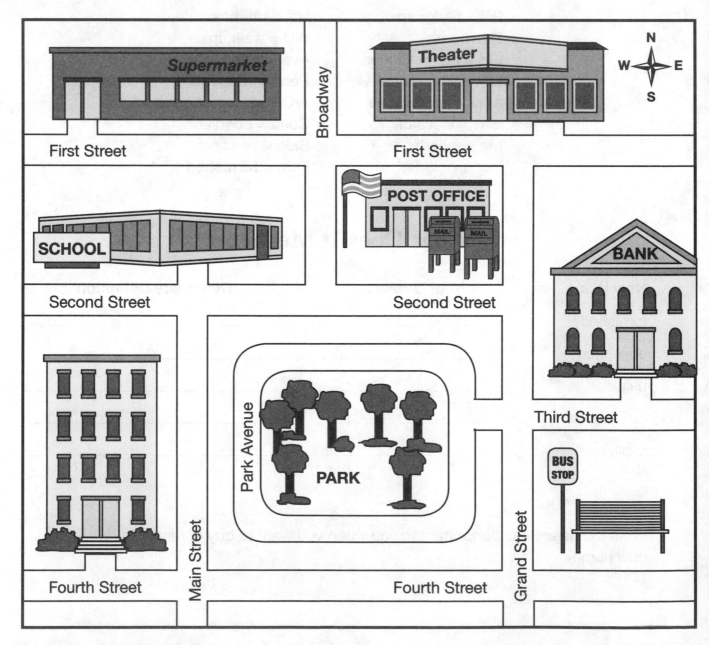

Apply What You've Learned

Choose two favorite places that people like to visit in your city or town. Tell the class why these places are special.

Draw a map showing each place. Mark each place with a small picture or symbol. On the map, show a partner the shortest route to get to each place from your school. Tell your partner the streets you go on and what places you pass to get there.

Write About You

Write about your experience finding a place to live in the U.S. How did you find your apartment or house? Why did you choose that place? Why did you choose your neighborhood?

_____

_____

_____

_____

_____

_____

_____

_____

_____

_____

_____

_____

_____

_____

_____

_____

_____

_____

_____

_____

_____

Changing Traditions

Customs are the ways people of
different countries and religions do
things. For example, people in Japan
bow when they meet someone. In
the U.S., people shake hands. What
surprised you the most about customs
in the U.S. when you first came to
this country?

Celebrating the Jewish Sabbath
(collection of the Lower East Side Tenement Museum)

Many Chinese immigrants come to the U.S. from Hong Kong. Lisa Cheng came to this country when she was a young woman. Her story shows how immigrants' cultures can affect their lives in the U.S.

In Hong Kong Lisa was poor. Her family rented a small room. They all lived together in that tiny space. Her father wanted to bring her to the U.S. He told Lisa that she was going to live in a big apartment with a living room, kitchen, and toilet inside. She was also going to have her own bedroom. Lisa was very excited. But when she got to New York City, she saw a tenement building and her tiny apartment. It was nothing like the apartment her father described. She was very sad.

But Lisa wanted to stay here and learn English. She used her dictionary every day to learn new words. She also wanted to learn about life and customs in the U.S. But she did not give up her Chinese culture to be an American. She added some American ways to her own culture. She didn't even change her name. Instead, she added the American name—Lisa—to her Chinese name.

Lisa thinks the family is the most important thing in Chinese culture. When she first came to New York, her great uncle helped her family settle in Chinatown. Her great aunt helped Lisa's mom find a job in a clothing factory. Lisa even worked there one summer to make money.

Lisa also has Chinese traditions she doesn't want to keep. In her culture, people respect the elderly. Young people must listen and obey everything the elderly say. If an older person says to do something in a particular way, then the younger person must listen. It doesn't matter what the younger person thinks. In the U.S., Lisa still respects her parents and older people. But if she disagrees with them for a good reason, then she will tell them and make her own decision. Lisa believes that to succeed in the U.S., she has to be open to American culture.

About the Story

1. How did Lisa's apartment in Hong Kong differ from her new apartment in New York City?

2. What was one important thing Lisa did to learn English?

3. In what ways did Lisa's relatives help her family adjust to life in the U.S.?

4. What did Lisa want to keep from her culture? What did she want to change?

5. What does Lisa think she needs to do in order to succeed in the U.S.?

What's Your Experience?

Lisa kept some Chinese customs and she gave up other ones. Did you keep customs from your own culture when you came to the U.S? If so, what were they? Did you give up any customs? If so, what were they? Why did you keep or give up the customs?

What Do You Think?

1. Lisa's father said the family was going to have a big apartment in the U.S. Do you think he really believed this?

2. Lisa really wanted to speak English. Why do you think this was so important to her?

3. Do you agree with Lisa's opinion about listening to the elderly?

Words You Can Use: Talking about Customs

Every country has different ways of doing things. These practices are called **customs**. You can be **embarrassed** if you do not know how people **behave** in a different **culture**. It is important to be **sensitive** to other people's customs. Behaviors that are **appropriate** in your native country may be **offensive** in another culture. It is important not to be **misunderstood**.

customs = traditions
behave = act
appropriate = correct
offensive = insulting or rude

embarrassed = uncomfortable or ashamed
culture = actions and beliefs of a large group
sensitive to = concerned about
misunderstood = not understood

Discuss: With a partner, talk about your experiences with customs in the U.S. Was there a time when you were embarrassed? Were you ever offended by someone? Are people in the U.S. sensitive to your culture? Have you ever been misunderstood?

Try It Out

Write a letter to a friend in your country. Tell him or her some things about U.S. culture. Use some of the words above to describe your experience.

How You Say It: Connector Words

Connector words can be used to join two or more complete sentences. Some are: *and, but, so,* and *or. And* and *or* can also join words and phrases.

- *And* adds more information.
  Example: I like pasta, *and* I like rice.
  I like pasta *and* rice.

- *But* shows contrasting information.
  Example: I like pasta, *but* I don't like rice.

- *So* gives a result or a consequence.
  Example: I like pasta, *so* I eat at many Italian restaurants.

- *Or* gives a choice.
  Example: We can order pasta, *or* we can order rice.
  We can order pasta *or* rice.

Try It Out
Write a sentence about yourself on each topic using *and, but, so,* and *or.* Use each connector word once.

Example: (language)
 I speak Russian, and I also speak Chinese. OR I speak Russian and Chinese.

1. language

_____

2. food

_____

3. family

_____

4. sports

_____

Put It Together

A. Are the following customs, behaviors, and practices the same or different in the U.S. from those in your native country? Check the appropriate box.

	Same	Different		Same	Different
Dating	☐	☐	Greetings	☐	☐
Men's clothing	☐	☐	Gift giving	☐	☐
Women's clothing	☐	☐	Tipping	☐	☐
Mealtime	☐	☐	Vacation time	☐	☐
Being on time	☐	☐			

B. Select five of the above customs. Compare the way they are done in your native country with the way they are done in the U.S. First say if the custom is the same or different in the U.S. Then, write about it using a connecting word.

Example: In South America we have a big meal at noontime, *but* in the U.S. we eat a big meal at night.
In France most people take vacations in August, *so* the beaches get very crowded then.

1. _____

_____

2. _____

_____

3. _____

_____

4. _____

_____

5. _____

_____

This is a story about marriage customs in the Confino family. The family came here from Greece and lived on Orchard Street.

Some of the words in the reading are in bold. Try to guess the meanings of these new words. Then find the meanings in a dictionary.

Marriage, Sephardic Style

Before 1900, in some cultures, parents decided who their children would marry. This custom was called an **arranged** marriage. Arranged marriages were a custom among Sephardic Jews for many years. (Sephardic Jews are the descendents of Jews who left Spain hundreds of years ago.) Girls usually married between the ages of 12 and 16. The bride's family had to **supply** money or expensive goods to the groom. This was called a dowry.

Victoria Confino's family was Sephardic. They lived in Greece. Her older sister, Allegra, was 16 when she married Sam Russo. Sam was born in Greece, but he moved to the U.S. When he was 24 years old, Sam returned to Greece to find a wife. Victoria's parents **selected** Sam as a husband for Allegra. At the wedding, Allegra cried. She did not want to leave her family and friends. She did not want to go to the U.S. with this **stranger**. When the couple arrived in New York City, they **settled** in an apartment at 97 Orchard Street.

What Does It Mean?

New Word	Your Guess	Dictionary Definition
arranged	_____	_____
supply	_____	_____
select	_____	_____
stranger	_____	_____
settle	_____	_____

Discuss
What are the marriage customs in your own culture? Do you think parents should decide who their children can marry? Do you think Allegra was too young to marry and move away from her family?

Picture It

A. With a partner, make a list of customs from your culture and a list of customs from your partner's culture.

My Culture   **My Partner's Culture**

_____   _____

_____   _____

_____   _____

_____   _____

_____   _____

_____   _____

_____   _____

B. Now use the Venn Diagram below. Write customs from your culture in the circle under My Culture. Have your partner write his or her customs in the circle under My Partner's Culture. In the area marked Both, write the customs you both have in common. Now you can see the similarities and differences.

My Culture   **My Partner's Culture**

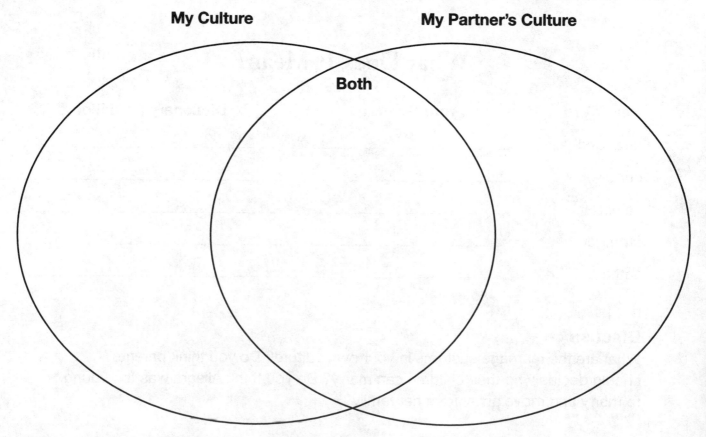

Both

Apply What You've Learned

Customs can be different in the U.S. and in your native country. Work in a group. Ask your classmates what they would do in the following situations. Take notes in the spaces below. Then report the results to the class.

1. You are a woman, and your name is Jane Smith. You marry a man named Mark Brown. Should your name become Jane Brown?

2. Your parents don't approve of the man or woman you want to marry. What should you do?

3. You have sent out invitations to your wedding and have arranged for the food, flowers, and music. The week before the wedding, you don't think you want to get married. What do you do?

4. How do you dress for a wedding in the U.S.? How do you dress for a wedding in your native country?

5. What are some good wedding gifts in the U.S.? What are traditional ones in your native country?

Write About You

Would you marry someone from a different culture or background? What are some of the good things about this kind of marriage? What could be some of the problems with it?

_____

_____

_____

_____

_____

_____

_____

_____

_____

_____

_____

_____

_____

_____

_____

_____

_____

_____

_____

_____

_____

LESSON 5

Feeding the Family

Your **diet** is the food you eat everyday.

One hundred years ago, people did

not eat the way we do today. Even

now, people all over the world have

different diets. What is your diet?

What did your grandparents eat?

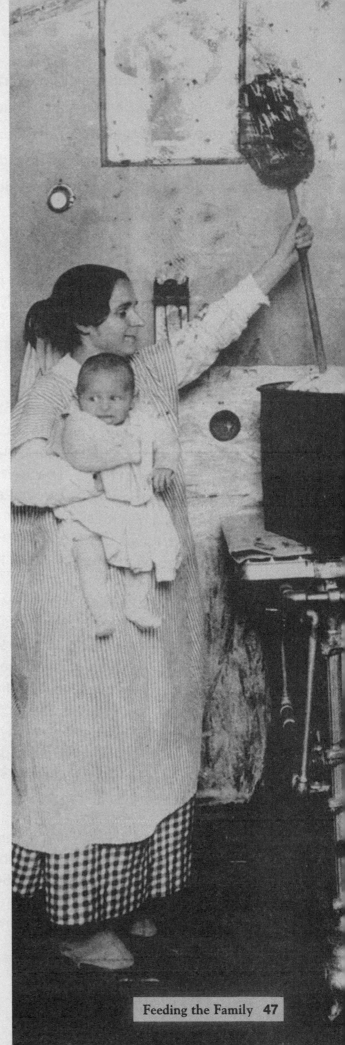

Washing diapers in a tenement kitchen,
around 1910
(collection of the National Archives)

Life for new immigrants on New York City's Lower East Side was very hard. Feeding the family was a big problem for everyone. The story of the De Santis family shows how difficult it was for people to buy and store food.

There were seven people in Concetta De Santis' family. In 1910 they came to the U.S. from Sicily, which is part of Italy. They settled on Allen Street, on New York City's Lower East Side. There, the family lived in a four-room apartment on the top floor.

Concetta's mother went to Orchard Street every day to buy the family's food. When Concetta was eight years old, she would go to the grocery store for a quart of milk. She carried her own pitcher from home. The store owner poured milk into it. She also paid 15 cents to buy butter and some rolls. That was the family's breakfast every morning. There was one tub in the kitchen. It was used to prepare food and wash clothes. The family also used it for weekly baths.

Concetta's family had an icebox. The icebox held food and a 20-pound piece of ice. The ice kept the food cold. In the winter, the family kept food outside on the windowsill or on the fire escape. Many families on the Lower East Side lived like the De Santis family. People didn't have refrigerators. In the winter, they put milk, cheese, eggs, and meat outside on the window sills. This kept the food cold. When it was warm outside, an iceman delivered a big piece of ice to the apartment. He put it in the icebox. Some pieces of ice weighed as much as 30 pounds.

The icebox cost less than five dollars. But that was a lot of money at the time. A pound of fresh butter cost 35 cents, and a 10-pound box of macaroni cost 54 cents. These foods were very expensive because most people only earned a little more than two dollars for a full day's work.

The kitchen of the Baldizzi apartment at 97 Orchard Street, recreated by the Lower East Side Tenement Museum (collection of the Lower East Side Tenement Museum)

About the Story

1. How did Concetta's family keep food cold in the summertime?

2. How did the De Santis family get fresh milk every day?

3. There was one large tub in the kitchen. What was this used for?

4. How did Concetta's mother feed the family?

5. What did an iceman do?

What's Your Experience?

The icebox was very useful 100 years ago. It made food storage easier for people. What do you have in your kitchen today to make life easier?

What Do You Think?

1. In the early 1900s, ice was very expensive for many people. Why do you think it cost so much? What do you think families did who could not afford Ice?

2. Why do you think Concetta had to carry her own pitcher to the store when she went to get milk?

3. What were the problems of shopping, cooking, and keeping food fresh for people living on New York City's Lower East Side?

Words You Can Use: Buying Food

When we describe some packaged foods or some kinds of fruits and vegetables, we can use the following words:

a *carton* of milk	a *box* of cereal
a *carton* of eggs	a *can* of soda
a *carton* of juice	a *can* of beans
a *bunch* of bananas	a *bag* of flour
a *head* of lettuce	a *box* of spaghetti
a *bottle* of soda	a *loaf* of bread
a *bottle* of ketchup	a *jar* of peanut butter

Discuss

How many of these packages or kinds of food do you have in your kitchen? Use the new words to tell your classmates what you have.

Try It Out

Make a shopping list of foods you need to buy. Use the list above. Include a number to show how many of each one you need. Add your own ideas if you need foods that are not on the list.

Shopping List

_____

_____

_____

_____

_____

_____

_____

_____

_____

How You Say It: Count and Noncount Nouns

Count nouns name things that can be counted. Use *a/an* before these words if they are singular. For example, *a* carrot, *an* apple, *a* supermarket. These words become plural by adding the letter *s* at the end. For example: *two carrots, three apples, four supermarkets.*

Noncount nouns name things that can't be counted. When we think of these things, we see them as a whole, not as separate units. Do not use *a* or *an* before these words. Do not put *s* at the end to make these words plural. For example: *milk, rice, sugar.*

Try It Out

Which of the following foods are countable and which are not countable? If the word is countable, write the word with *a/an* for the singular form and add an *s* for the plural form. Put an *X* on the lines if the word is not countable.

	Singular	**Plural**
1. apple	an apple	apples
2. pasta		
3. orange		
4. coffee		
5. juice		
6. fish		
7. bread		
8. ice cream		
9. onion		
10. cake		

Put It Together

A. Work with a partner. Ask and answer the following questions. Write notes about your partner's answers. Share the answers with the class.

1. What is your favorite food from your native country?

2. What food don't you like to eat?

3. What are some foods that are healthy to eat?

4. What foods do you like to cook?

5. What is your favorite new food in the U.S.?

B. Imagine you are making a special dinner for a friend or family member. Write a story about the meal you will serve. Write about your trip to the supermarket and what you are going to buy there. Describe the dinner you are going to eat. Share your story with the class.

_____

_____

_____

_____

_____

_____

_____

_____

_____

_____

_____

_____

This is the story of a traditional meal eaten by Jewish immigrants. After you read the story, look at the bold words. Then choose the word that goes with each meaning below.

A Traditional Meal

On cold winter days, immigrants often ate **stews**. These stews **reflected** the culture of the immigrants' native countries. They were usually made from old family **recipes**. Religious Jews could not turn their ovens on or off during the Sabbath. The Sabbath began on Friday night and ended at sundown on Saturday night. These immigrants often made a **traditional** dish called *cholent*. It was a popular dish because it could be cooked overnight. On Friday night, women turned on the stove. They placed the pot in the oven. The stew cooked until Saturday evening. After sundown, women turned off the oven and served cholent to **celebrate** the end of the Sabbath.

What Is the Word?

Look in the story to find these vocabulary words.

1. Find the word that means *to do something special*. _____

2. Find the word that means *to show or express something*. _____

3. Find the word for *instructions on how to cook something*. _____

4. Find the word that means *following an old custom*. _____

5. Find the name of *a meal cooked in a big pot*. _____

Discuss
What are some traditional dishes from your native country? Do people eat these dishes for special occasions, or are they everyday food?

Picture It

Supermarkets in the U.S. have many different places to find food. Look at the diagram below. It shows some sections, or aisles, of a supermarket.

Where would you find the following items? Write the names under the correct supermarket aisle.

bananas	eggs	onions
bottled water	frozen dinners	paper towels
broccoli	granola	potatoes
butter	hamburger patties	salmon
canned soup	ice cream	a sandwich
cold cereal	milk	soda
donuts	noodles	watermelon
eggplant	oatmeal	yogurt

Dairy

Bakery

Frozen Foods

Beverages

Breakfast Foods

Canned Goods

Meat

Deli

Pasta and Rice

Produce (Fruits and Vegetables)

Apply What You've Learned

On the cards below, write a recipe for a dish that you remember from your childhood. Share your recipe with the class. Tell about your memories of this dish.

What food is needed—Ingredients

_____

_____

_____

_____

_____

_____

_____

How to make it—Instructions

_____

_____

_____

_____

_____

_____

_____

Write About You

How is eating different in the U.S. than in your own country? Write about how you shop for food, what you eat, when you eat, and who you eat with.

_____

_____

_____

_____

_____

_____

_____

_____

_____

_____

_____

_____

_____

_____

_____

_____

_____

_____

_____

_____

_____

LESSON 6

Shopping on a Budget

A **budget** is a plan that helps you use your money wisely. To make a **budget**, you need to know how much money you make and how much money you spend on necessities. What are some items that you pay for each month, like rent and food? Think about how much you spend on those items. Do you have money left at the end of the month?

Orchard Street on Manhattan's Lower East Side in 1939
(photograph by David Berkowitz; collection of the Lower East Side Tenement Museum)

Shopping on a Budget **57**

Shopping was an important part of life for new immigrants on New York City's Lower East Side. They did not have big supermarkets or shopping malls. Most of the shopping and selling was done everyday in the streets. This story describes what shopping was like on the Lower East Side almost 100 years ago.

Shoppers on on Manhattan's Lower East Side, around 1948
(photograph by Donald Sheppard; collection of the Lower East Side Tenement Museum)

Orchard Street was a very colorful place. Every morning the neighborhood women walked to Orchard Street to shop. In those days, there were no plastic bags, and leather bags were very expensive. The women carried their own shopping bags made out of oilcloth. These bags were very strong and could be carried in the rain or snow. Everything the women bought went into these bags.

Both sides of Orchard Street were filled from end to end with pushcarts. Many men were peddlers. Peddlers called out to the crowds. They told people to buy their goods. There was so much noise that people had to yell to be heard. Each peddler sold a different item. One peddler was selling soup greens; another one was selling bananas; another one was selling cantaloupes. Women went from pushcart to pushcart to fill up their shopping bags.

There were also many different kinds of stores. Store owners sold clothing, brooms, sponges, dry foods, soap, cloth, and many other items. Outside the stores, many owners hung samples to show what was inside the store. These samples hung high over the heads of the shoppers on Orchard Street. This made the street look very crowded, but also very lively.

Many people lived in the buildings above the stores. Families with their children used to sit on their fire escapes in the summertime. They looked down at the busy streets and watched all the activities. It was something special to see.

About the Story

1. Why did women carry their own shopping bags when they went shopping?

2. Describe the kinds of things people sold and bought on Orchard Street.

3. Why was there so much noise on Orchard Street? What was going on there?

4. How did store owners try to get people to buy their goods?

5. What was good and what was bad about living in the buildings above the stores?

What's Your Experience?

Compare shopping on New York City's Lower East Side to shopping in your native country. Think about what you can buy, how people shop, where people shop, and how people get their purchases home.

What Do You Think?

1. Going shopping was a big part of people's lives 100 years ago. A trip to Orchard Street meant more to people than just buying goods. Why do you think the people in that neighborhood liked to go shopping?

2. One hundred years ago, many store owners displayed products outside their stores to let people know what they had. Do store owners still do that? How do they attract shoppers now?

3. Children and families liked to watch all the activities on Orchard Street. Today, we call this *people watching.* Why do you think this was a popular activity?

Words You Can Use: Going Shopping

Here are some everyday words people use when they go shopping or talk about shopping.

bargains	discount
charge	exchange
coupon	receipt
credit card	refund
department stores	shopping list

Complete the sentences below with one of the words from the box.

Example: I love to shop in _department stores_. They have everything I need.

1. I'm out of milk. I must remember to put it on my _____.

2. This sweater is too small. I'll have to _____ it for a larger one.

3. After Christmas, you can get a lot of _____ because there are many sales.

4. I used a _____ at the supermarket to get 10% off of the price.

5. I don't have enough cash, so I'll _____ my purchases.

6. You can't return merchandise without a _____.

7. If you return an item in seven days, you can get a full _____.

8. If you lose your _____, you must call the company to cancel it and send you a new one.

9. Some _____ stores sell items for less money.

How You Say It: Verb + Preposition

We often use certain verbs and prepositions together. The more you repeat these verb + preposition combinations, the easier it will be for you to remember them. Below is a list of some verb + preposition combinations that can be used when you go shopping. Do you know what these phrases mean? If not, most native speakers will be able to explain them to you.

look at	take off
look for	pay for
think about	wait on
decide on	help out
try on	put on

Try It Out

Talk with a partner. Ask and answer the questions using the verb phrases in parentheses. You and your partner may have different answers.

Example: Question: What do you do in a clothing store? *(try on)*
        Answer: I try on clothes.

1. What does a salesperson do in a store? *(wait on)*

2. What do you do in a shoe store? *(try on)*

3. What does a customer do at the checkout counter? *(pay for)*

4. What do you do in a dressing room? *(take off)*

5. What do you do when you walk by a store window? *(look at)*

6. What do you do if you can't decide what to buy? *(think about)*

7. What do you do with new clothes when you get home? *(put on)*

8. What do you do when you can't find an item in a store? *(look for)*

Put It Together

Work with a partner. Pretend you are in a clothing store. One of you is the customer. One of you is the salesperson. The customer is looking for new clothes. Write what the customer and salesperson are saying to each other. Use as many verb phrases and vocabulary words as you can. After you have finished, read the dialogue to the class.

Salesperson: _____

_____

Customer: _____

_____

Salesperson: _____

_____

Customer: _____

_____

Salesperson: _____

_____

Customer: _____

_____

Salesperson: _____

_____

Customer: _____

_____

Salesperson: _____

_____

Customer: _____

_____

Lilli Marcus grew up on Orchard Street. This story tells about how she went shopping for her mother and how she spent her money.

Some of the words in the reading are in bold. Try to guess the meanings of these new words. Then find the meanings in a dictionary.

Shopping on Orchard Street

When Lilli went shopping for milk, her mother gave her a metal **pitcher** and some money. Lilli walked downstairs to the **basement** of her tenement. There was a small grocery store there. She asked the grocer to pour five cents worth of milk into the pitcher. There were also lots of bakeries on the street. Lilli could go and buy a roll for one or two cents. Two cookies cost one penny. A **slice** of cheese also cost a penny or two. Lilly spent the rest of her money on crackers. Three or four crackers only cost one penny. A box cost two or three cents.

After she bought crackers, Lilli and her friends sat on boxes in front of their house and ate them. She still remembers the smells from the pickle stands on the street. Everything smelled **delicious**. Outside her home, she often bought a roll and two frankfurters with mustard and sauerkraut for five cents. She used to **wrap up** the frankfurter and take it into the movies so that she could eat and watch the movies at the same time.

Lilli was poor, but happy. She had good memories of her childhood on Orchard Street.

What Does It Mean?

New Word	Your Guess	Dictionary Definition
pitcher	_____	_____
basement	_____	_____
slice	_____	_____
delicious	_____	_____
wrap up	_____	_____

Discuss

In the early 1900s, people didn't earn much money. A penny could buy a lot more than it can today. When you came to the U.S., did you have enough money to buy what you wanted? What prices surprised you?

Picture It

Here are six different kinds of stores. Under each store, write five items that the store sells. Put a check (✓) next to items that you have bought from each type of store.

Clothing Store

sweaters

Hardware Store

nails

Electronic Store

radio

Appliance Store

refrigerator

Drugstore

shampoo

Sporting Goods Store

soccer ball

Apply What You've Learned

The table below lists how much everyday items cost per week for a family of four in 1874 on New York City's Lower East Side.

In the column on the right, write what you think these items cost now for a family of four.

Item	Cost ($) in 1874	Cost ($) now
Flour and bread	.84	
Meats	2.82	
Butter	.50	
Cheese	.22	
Sugar	.34	
Milk	.49	
Coffee	.19	
Tea	.25	
Fish	.15	
Soap	.40	
Eggs	.25	
Vegetables	1.00	
Fruits	.28	
Fuel for cooking	1.00	
School supplies	.15	
Clothing	1.79	

Discuss

In the late 1800s, most people on New York City's Lower East Side earned about $2.26 a day for work and spent about $3.75 a week on rent. If you lived at 97 Orchard Street in 1874 and worked six days a week, how would you spend your money? Compare your ideas with a partner.

Write About You

If you had a thousand dollars, how would you spend it? How would you spend a million dollars?

_____

_____

_____

_____

_____

_____

_____

_____

_____

_____

_____

_____

_____

_____

_____

_____

_____

_____

_____

_____

_____

_____

_____

LESSON 7

Staying Healthy

Health refers to the condition of your body or mind. If you take good care of yourself, you have a better chance of being in good health, or **healthy**. There are many health problems in different parts of the world. What is the biggest health problem in your native country? What do people do about that problem?

In the early 1900s, healthcare was expensive, and many diseases could not be cured. Tuberculosis was a dangerous disease of the lungs. It was very contagious, so many people caught it from each other. Lily Merman was born on New York City's Lower East Side in the early 1900s. In this story, she describes her father's illness and death.

The immigrants on New York City's Lower East Side had many hardships. The garbage, the pollution, and the rats made people sick. People became ill with contagious diseases such as tuberculosis. Some died. These diseases spread easily to family members, because families lived and slept together in small, crowded rooms. Doctors at the time knew little about these diseases. They often told the patients to take medicine that didn't work. The air was not good on the Lower East Side. There were almost no trees or grass. Doctors told their sick patients to go to the mountains to breathe fresh air. But no one had enough money to leave the city. Many people turned to religion and prayed for their health.

One day, Lily Merman's father learned he had tuberculosis. At that time, there was no cure. People who got the disease knew they were going to die. Lily's mother rushed her husband to the doctor. The doctor told him he needed fresh air and had to go to the mountains. He also told Lily's mother to get medicine.

That day, Lily's mother went to the corner drugstore to buy medicine for her husband. When she returned, it was too late. Lily's father had died on a small bed in the living room. His three daughters and son were with him. Lily's father was 39 years old when he died. Her mother was only 28 years old. She was left with four children. They were 3, 4, 6, and 10 years old.

Without a father, Lily, her sisters, and her brother had a hard time getting an education. They had to work at low-paying jobs to help support the family. Finally, the family was able to leave the Lower East Side. Unlike many others, Lily and her brother and sisters were lucky. They did not catch tuberculosis from their father.

About the Story

1. Many people got sick living in the tenements. Explain why this happened.

2. Often, people from the same family got sick with the same disease. How did this happen?

3. Doctors told people with tuberculosis to go to the mountains. Why did doctors think going to the mountains would help people with this disease?

4. Why did people turn to religion when they got sick with tuberculosis or other serious diseases?

5. After Lily's father died, the family's life changed. In what ways did life became different for the children?

What's Your Experience?

Today tuberculosis is considered a curable disease. However, we have other medical problems, such as expensive health insurance and new diseases that can't be easily cured. In your native country, where do people go when they get sick? What do you do when you are sick in the U.S.? Who pays for your medical care?

What Do You Think?

1. Tuberculosis was a very serious illness for people 100 years ago, before doctors had a cure for it. What are some of the most serious diseases today?

2. Lily's father died at home with his family around him. This was common many years ago. Today, many people die apart from their family. They are in hospitals or other medical care facilities. Which way do you think is better, and why?

3. Lily's mother was only 28 years old when her husband died. What do you think her life was like? What problems do you think she had being a single mother?

Words You Can Use: Parts of the Body

When you are sick, it is important to know how to tell a friend, a doctor, or a pharmacist what is the matter.

Label the drawing with the body parts listed. If you do not know a word, ask your teacher or classmate to point to the body part on the drawing.

Head	Leg (legs)	Shoulder (shoulders)
Foot (feet)	Neck	Arm (arms)
Eye (eyes)	Throat	Hand (hands)
Nose	Stomach	Ear (ears)
Chest	Mouth	Back

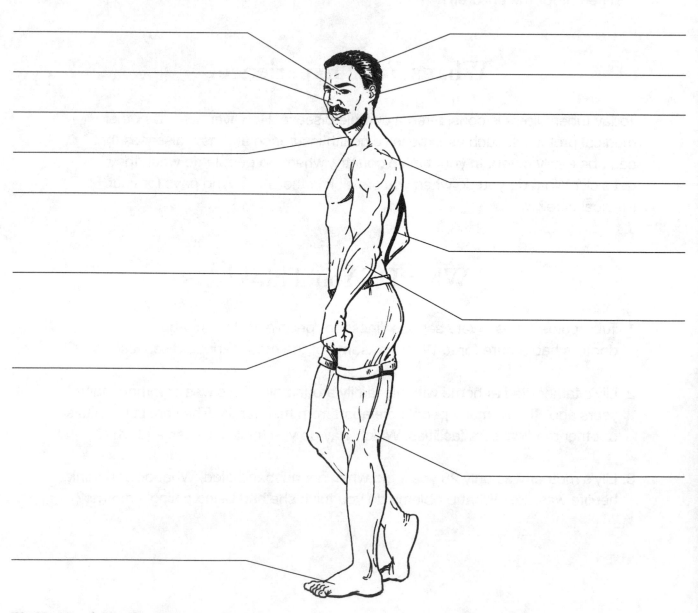

How You Say It: Modals

Modals are helping verbs—words that modify verbs. Some modals are used to give advice. Different modals indicate different kinds of advice.

- Use the words *have to* or *must* with verbs to indicate that someone has no choice.
  Example: If you break your leg, you *have to* go to the hospital.
  If you have pains in your chest, you *must* call your doctor.

- Use the word *should* when you want to give strong advice.
  Example: If you feel dizzy, you *should* lie down.
  If you are hungry, you *should* eat something.

- Use *could* or *can* when the advice is not as strong as *should*. *Could* and *can* usually mean the person has more choice about what to do.
  Example: If you can't sleep, you *could* drink a cup of hot milk.
  If you are overweight, you *can* cut out sweets, and you *can* exercise.

Try It Out

Give advice to someone who has a bad cold. Use the modals above to tell them what they *should, could, can, must,* or *have to* do. Write your advice on the lines below. Discuss your ideas with the class.

_____

_____

_____

_____

_____

_____

_____

_____

Put It Together

Use one or more modals to tell someone what to do for the following health problems. Write your ideas below. Compare your ideas with the class.

Example: Problem: backache
    Advice: You *must* not lift heavy boxes. You *could* call the doctor.
        You *should* put ice on your back. You *could* get a massage.

1. Problem: stomachache

_____

_____

2. Problem: insomnia (inability to sleep)

_____

_____

3. Problem: a cut on the knee

_____

_____

4. Problem: a fever of over 104 degrees

_____

_____

5. Problem: dry skin

_____

_____

6. Problem: bad chest pains

_____

_____

7. Problem: nausea or upset stomach

_____

_____

In the 1890s most women had their babies at home, without a doctor. Women called midwives helped many mothers have their children. This is the story of the work midwives did.

Some of the words in the reading are in bold. Try to guess the meanings of these new words. Then find the meanings in a dictionary.

Midwives

In the 1890s, most couples did not have enough money to have a doctor **deliver** their babies. Instead most women had their babies at home, with the help of midwives.

Midwives were not **trained** in hospitals but had a lot of **experience**. They arrived at the mother's home with a special bag. Inside was a strong soap for the midwife to wash her hands and the mother's body. The bag also held scissors to cut the baby's **umbilical cord**, a thin rope or tape to tie the cord, cotton, and petroleum jelly. Midwives could take care of most problems. Sometimes they had to call a doctor because they could not do **surgery**.

Midwives had to wash their hands for five minutes. They also had to boil all their tools before they delivered the baby. After the birth, the midwife came to the mother's house for several days. She helped with cleaning, laundry, shopping, and cooking. She also checked up on the health of the mother and her baby.

What Does It Mean?

New Word	Your Guess	Dictionary Definition
deliver	_____	_____
train	_____	_____
experience	_____	_____
umbilical cord	_____	_____
surgery	_____	_____

Discuss
Where do women go to have babies in your native country? Who helps them with the birth? Who helps them at home after the baby is born?

Picture It

There are many ways to stay healthy. In the circles below, write different ways to stay healthy. Add details in the smaller circles. Add more lines and circles if you need them.

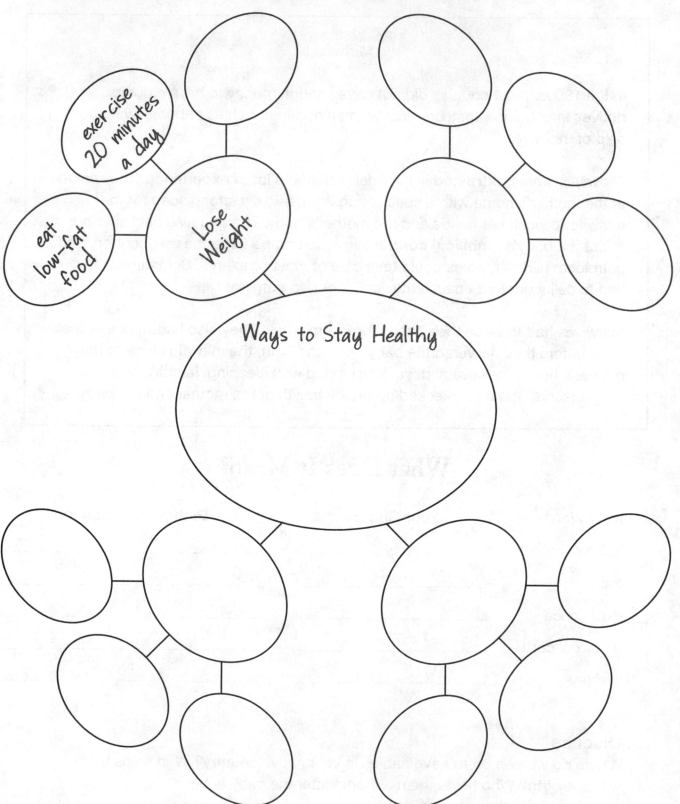

Ways to Stay Healthy

exercise 20 minutes a day

eat low-fat food

Lose Weight

Apply What You've Learned

Here are some words you may find on a medicine label.

Prescription A doctor's written order for use of medicine

Dosage Amount of medicine a person should take

Directions How and when to take the medicine

Use as directed Follow the directions from your doctor

Warnings Be aware of these possible problems

Do not exceed Do not take more than this amount

Expiration (Exp.) Do not use after this date

External Use Only Do not swallow or put in eyes, ears, or nose, or inside any other body part

Overdose Too much of the medicine

OTC Over the counter; medicine you can get without a prescription

PAIN-AWAY OTC
Pain Reliever/Fever Reducer Tablets

Uses: Gives temporary relief of minor aches and pain caused by headache, toothache, the common cold, backache, mentrual cramps, minor arthritis. Also for temporary reduction of fever.

Directions: Adults and children 12 years and older: take 1 or 2 tablets every 4 to 6 hours as needed, with water. Do not exceed 8 tablets in 24 hours unless directed by a doctor. Not recommended for children under 12 years of age.

Warnings: Do not take this product for more than 10 days for pain or more than 3 days for fever unless directed by a doctor. If pain or fever persists or gets worse, or if new symptoms occur, consult a doctor. May cause allergic reaction, including rash or hives, swelling, wheezing, or shock. Do not use this if you have had an allergic reaction to another pain reliever or fever reducer. Stop using the product and get medical attention immediately if an allergic reaction occurs. If you are pregnant or nursing, do not use this product.

Alcohol warning: If you consume 3 or more alcoholic drinks per day, consult your doctor before taking this or any pain other reliever or fever reducer.

Keep this and all drugs out of the reach of children.

In case of accidental overdose, contact a doctor or poison control center immediately.

Try It Out
Read the label. Answer the questions below. Compare answers with a partner. Tell how you knew each answer.

1. *Could* you get this medicine without a prescription?
2. *Should* you take this drug if you are pregnant?
3. *Should* you drink alcohol with this drug?
4. What is the maximum dose an adult *should* take in one day?
5. What is the maximum number of days you *should* take this medicine before contacting your doctor?
6. For what three health problems *could* you use this medicine?
7. What dosage *should* you give a 12-year-old child?

Write About You

Write about a time you were sick or didn't feel well. What was the matter? What did you do to get better? What do you do now (or try to do) to stay healthy?

_____

_____

_____

_____

_____

_____

_____

_____

_____

_____

_____

_____

_____

_____

_____

_____

_____

_____

_____

_____

_____

_____

LESSON 8

Working for a Living

Employment means work or how you earn a living. What kind of employment did you have in your native country? Have you been able to do the same work in the U.S.?

Rosaria Baldizzi, pictured seated, second from the left, at work in a garment factory
(collection of the Lower East Side Tenement Museum)

Many immigrants think they will have an easy time finding a job in the U.S. The truth is that it can be difficult to find a job. It can be even more difficult to adjust to the work schedule. Solomon Confino and Anselmo Zanes are examples of immigrants who had difficulty finding good jobs in the U.S.

Solomon Confino arrived in the U.S. in 1957. He came from Greece. Before he came here, there was a big earthquake in Greece. The U.S. government let many Greeks come to this country, and Solomon was one of them. But he also came to escape religious discrimination. In addition, he wanted a better job and a chance to build a family.

When Solomon arrived, he met other Greek immigrants. People from Cyprus helped him find a job. His first job was in a restaurant, washing dishes at night. Two weeks later he got a second job in another restaurant. He worked there during the day. Later, he went to school to learn English. He had to work at night to earn money. One day, a friend gave him a part-time job in a bread bakery. Later he got a full-time job there. He worked at the bakery for a year and a half. He was surprised that he earned much more money than he did in Greece. At last, he went to a trade school to learn to be a mechanic. He learned about this school from other Greek friends. Finally, Solomon found a job as a mechanic.

Anselmo Zanes is an immigrant from Mexico. He now works as a janitor in a movie theatre. But his first job was very hard. He worked 17 hours a day in a sweatshop, from nine o'clock in the morning to two o'clock the next morning. He worked seven days a week, and only earned $75 a week. He did not know that his employer was cheating him. Anselmo should have gotten over $5.00 an hour. This was the minimum wage.

Like Anselmo, many immigrants work more than 12 hours a day and receive very low pay. One reason they may work for so little money is because they don't understand work laws in the U.S. They may not know about minimum wage laws. They may not know how many hours they should work. They also may not know where they can go to learn English and get a better job.

About the Story

1. Solomon thought the U.S. would be a good place to find work. What made him believe this?

2. Why were Solomon's first jobs in restaurants?

3. What are some reasons Solomon gave up his day job to go to school to learn English?

4. Why did Anselmo work so many hours?

5. What U.S. laws are important for immigrants like Anselmo? Why don't many immigrants know about these laws?

What's Your Experience?

Solomon Confino thought he would have a better job and life in the U.S. What job did you have in your native country? Before you came here, what kind of job did you think you would have? Is your job here better or worse than what you did in your native country? How is it similar or different?

What Do You Think?

1. Speaking English was very important for Solomon and Anselmo. What problems might immigrants have if they don't speak English?

2. Solomon's friends helped him find new jobs. What do you think are good ways to find jobs?

3. Anselmo may have worked long hours because he didn't know the law. What can a worker do if he or she feels the boss is not following the law?

Words You Can Use: Finding a Job

Help Wanted ads appear in the *Classified* or *Help Wanted* section of your newspaper. The newspaper uses shortened words, or abbreviations, to describe a job.

Asst = assistant	Immed = immediate
BA = college degree	K = thousand
Bfts = benefits	Nec = necessary
Dept = department	Oppty = opportunity
EOE = equal opportunity employer	Pref'd = preferred
Exec = executive	P/T = part time
Exc = excellent	Ref = references
Exp = experience	Req = required
F/T = full time	Sal = salary
Hrs = hours	Wk = work
HS = high school	WPM = words per minute (typing)

Look at the sample *Help Wanted* ad below. Answer the questions about this ad.

> **Restaurant Worker** Good oppty. F/T Asst. to chef. Immed. Tu-Sun 5-11 PM Wk. exp and HS req. Sal 15K + bfts. Fax resume & refs. to: Mr. Smith 718-555-1212

1. What job is advertised? _____

2. What qualifications do applicants need? _____

3. What is the salary? _____

4. What are the days and hours of work? _____

5. What is the starting date? _____

6. Whom does an applicant contact, and how? _____

7. What does an applicant have to send? _____

How You Say It: Frequency Adverbs

Frequency adverbs describe how often something happens. Listed below are some frequency adverbs. They begin with *always*—the word that means all of the time—and end with *never*—the word that means none of the time.

Always = 100% of the time
Usually = around 90% of the time
Often = 70 to 80% of the time
Sometimes = around 50% of the time
Occasionally = around 20% of the time
Seldom = around 5% of the time
Never = 0% of the time

Try It Out

Complete the following sentences about your work. Use one of the frequency adverbs. There is more than one possible answer. Share your answers with the class. If you don't work, change the sentences so you write about your ESL program.

Example: I _____*always*_____ work hard.

1. I _____ work hard at my job.

2. I _____ work in more than one place.

3. I _____ like my boss.

4. I _____ get along with my co-workers.

5. I _____ use a computer at work.

6. I _____ speak English at work.

7. I _____ use my native language at work.

8. I _____ have to talk on the phone at my job.

Put It Together

A. Below is a list of jobs and one task that workers might do in each one. Write a sentence using a frequency adverb to describe how often the worker does the task. Circle the adverb.

Example: Secretary/answers the phone

A secretary (always) answers the phone.

1. Receptionist/types letters

_____

2. Bus driver/stops at a red light

_____

3. Taxi driver/works at night

_____

4. Soccer player/scores points

_____

5. Manager/opens the mail

_____

6. Waiter/washes dishes

_____

B. Write a paragraph about the work you do. Tell about some tasks you do in your job. Try to use at least three frequency words. If you don't work, tell about tasks you do at home.

_____

_____

_____

_____

_____

_____

_____

Work conditions for many immigrants were very difficult at the turn of the century. This reading describes some of those conditions around 100 years ago.

Some of the words in the reading are in bold. Try to guess the meanings of these new words. Then find the meanings in a dictionary.

Working Life for Immigrants

In the early 1900s, many immigrants worked in crowded factories. These were called "sweatshops" because there was little **ventilation** in the rooms. Many men and women had to work for these companies because there were no other jobs. They often worked 14-hour days. They had no **benefits** or vacation time. Often, workers such as tailors, garment workers, and **unskilled** janitors could find work only seven or eight months a year.

Wages were also terrible. In the late 1800s, unskilled workers frequently earned only $1.75 for a 10-hour day. Many earned only $9 for a 60-hour work week.

Most working women had a double **burden**. In addition to their jobs, they had to take care of their families and homes. Wives shopped for food every day. They made lunch that their husbands took to work and cooked family meals early in the morning and late in the evening. They also cleaned the house, did the laundry, and made the family's clothes. (Among the poor in the 19th century, usually only men's outer clothing was purchased.) Many women also **managed** all the family money. Some women had jobs outside the house. Often, women cooked and sewed at home for pay.

What Does It Mean?

New Word	Your Guess	Dictionary Definition
ventilation	_____	_____
benefits	_____	_____
unskilled	_____	_____
burden	_____	_____
managed	_____	_____

Discuss
Who do you think had a more difficult work life 100 years ago—a man or a woman? Why? What about today?

Picture It

When do you work—during the day or night? Fill in the appropriate time clock(s). Write what you are doing for each hour that you are working. You can write about a job outside the home or about work that you do at home.

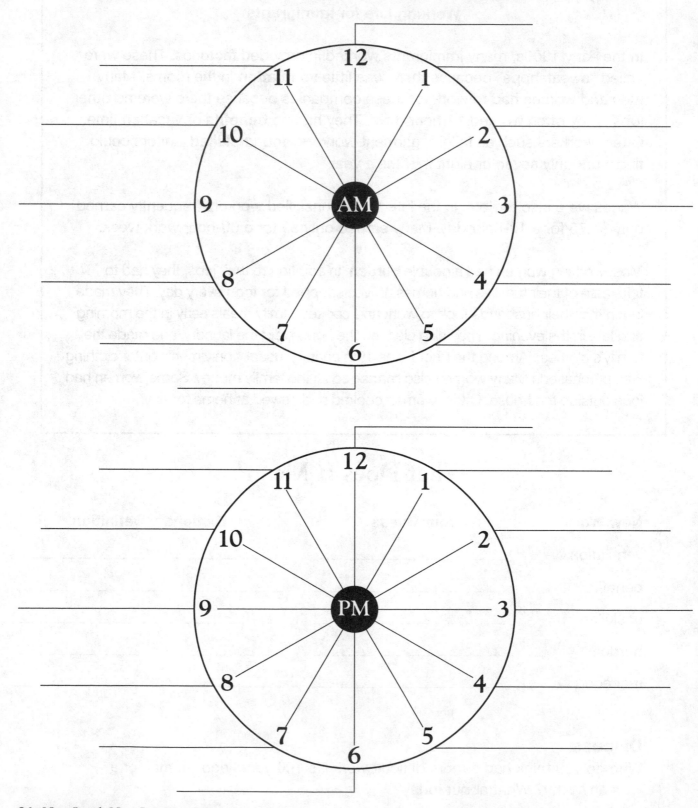

Apply What You've Learned

Bring a newspaper into class. Look in the *Help Wanted* section. Circle some jobs you would like to have. Then choose one of them for this activity.

Use the chart below to see if this is the job for you. In the first column, list your skills, your experience, and when you can work. In the second column, list the job requirements. Write the name or kind of job at the top of the column.

Me	Job: _____
_____	_____
_____	_____
_____	_____
_____	_____
_____	_____
_____	_____
_____	_____
_____	_____
_____	_____
_____	_____
_____	_____
_____	_____
_____	_____
_____	_____
_____	_____
_____	_____

Write About You

Immigrants had a very difficult time at work 100 years ago. Imagine you were an immigrant on New York City's Lower East Side at that time. Describe your workday and your feelings about it.

_____

_____

_____

_____

_____

_____

_____

_____

_____

_____

_____

_____

_____

_____

_____

_____

_____

_____

_____

_____

_____

_____

_____

_____

Fitting In

Discrimination is the practice of treating people unfairly because of their race, religion, sex, age, or nationality. Does discrimination exist in your native country? If so, what kind? Did you or members of your family experience it? If so, explain how you were unfairly treated.

Anti-immigration political cartoon
(Literary Digest, 1921; collection of the Lower East Side Tenement Museum)

Many immigrants experience discrimination in the U.S. because they seem different and have difficulty with English. This is the story of José Gil, an immigrant from the Dominican Republic.

José Gil was born in the countryside in the Dominican Republic. He had seven brothers and one sister. His family was very poor. Their house had no shower or toilet. José was going to be a rural teacher. This was not an important position in his country.

José decided to come to the U.S. for many reasons. He wanted a good education and a good job. He also wanted to have a family. José had a dream of helping other Dominicans in the U.S. He wanted to help them to improve their community. Sometimes José did not have hope of fulfilling his goals. While he was in the Dominican Republic, he listened to the Voice of America on the radio at night. He knew he had to learn English and understand U.S. culture.

Finally, José got a scholarship to study architecture at The City University of New York in New York City. He lived with a family in a large apartment in the city. He thought everything would be easy once he got to the U.S. But José was wrong. He still had a lot of problems in school. He understood English, but school was difficult. A professor told him he did not have any ability for architecture. The professor said that José should look for another career. José disagreed. He said he was going to finish his studies. José graduated in 1986 and became a college teacher. Eventually he taught alongside the same professor who said that he could not succeed.

Now, as a businessperson, José has worked mostly for small, minority-owned companies. He doesn't believe Dominicans have the same chance to succeed in large U.S. corporations. In order for José and other Dominicans to say, "I'm an American," he knows it is important to be accepted as part of the majority. That is not the case so far.

About the Story

1. Why did José want to leave his country to come to the U.S.? How did he prepare to come here?

2. What was José's dream for other Dominicans in the U.S.?

3. Why didn't José change careers when his professor said he had no ability for architecture?

4. Describe the type of company that has employed José. Why has he worked for this type of company?

5. How does José feel about being an American?

What's Your Experience?

José's story shows that minorities are not always accepted by people in the U.S. because of their country of birth, the color of their skin, or their language difficulties. Did you ever have problems in the U.S. for these reasons? Describe your experiences. Why do you think that some people in the U.S. treat others unfairly?

What Do You Think?

1. Is the U.S. a good place for José Gil? Discuss why you think it is or isn't.

2. José stayed in school even though it was difficult for him. What does this show about José's character?

3. If you wrote a letter to José, what are three questions you would like to ask him?

Words You Can Use: Adjectives

Here are words that describe people. How many of the words do you know?
Look up words you don't know in a dictionary.

Hair	Hair Color	Body Size	Eye Color
long	brown	tall	blue
short	blonde	short	brown
curly	black	fat	green
straight	red	thin	hazel
bald	grey	average	
	white		

Looks	Age	Personality
handsome	young	friendly
pretty	teen-aged	sensitive
attractive	middle-aged	serious
unattractive	old	shy
beautiful		energetic
sexy		happy
ugly		talkative
		fun-loving

Try It Out

Many adjectives can be used together to describe one person.

Example: He is a tall, attractive, middle-aged man.

Write one sentence about yourself using adjectives from the list. Write another
sentence about a person in your class using adjectives from the list.

Me

_____

_____

My Classmate

_____

_____

How You Say It: Comparisons

We can use adjectives to compare objects and people, to show how they are alike or different.

- If the adjective has one syllable, add -er to the adjective and follow it with the word *than*.
  Example: (short) José is **shorter than** Hector.

- If the adjective has two or more syllables and does not end in -y use *more* or *less* plus the adjective, followed by *than.*
  Example: (talkative) Mohammad is **more talkative than** John.
    John is **less talkative than** Mohammad.

- For adjectives ending in -y, change the -y to *i* and add -er.
  Example: (pretty) Hong is **prettier than** her friend.

- Some adjectives have different comparative forms. For example, the comparative of *good* is *better,* and the comparative of *bad* is *worse.*
  Example: José Gil's life in the U.S. is **better than** his life was in the Dominican Republic.
    José Gil's life in the Dominican Republic was **worse than** his life is in the U.S.

Try It Out
José Gil left the Dominican Republic for a better life in the U.S.
Write five sentences that describe how José's life in the U.S. is different from his life in the Dominican Republic. Use the following adjectives: *poor, optimistic, difficult, easy, and sad.*

Example: José was **poorer** in the Dominican Republic **than** he is in the U.S.

_____

_____

_____

_____

_____

Put It Together

On the lines below, write the name of the country where you were born.
Find a classmate or friend from a different country. Write sentences about
the topics below to compare your native countries. Use comparative words.
Use these adjectives or your own ideas:

busy	dangerous	hot	safe
cheap	delicious	humid	spacious
clean	dirty	peaceful	spicy
cloudy	dry	poor	sunny
cold	expensive	rainy	tasty
crowded	friendly	rude	warm

Your Country: _____

Partner's Country: _____

Example: Food: <u>The food in India is spicier than the food in Ireland.</u>

Size: _____

_____

Climate: _____

_____

Economy: _____

_____

Food: _____

_____

Crime: _____

_____

There are many different kinds of discrimination. These stories tell about people who have experienced discrimination.

Some of the words in the reading are in bold. Try to guess the meanings of these new words. Then find the meanings in a dictionary.

Discrimination

Mr. Anderson is a 60-year-old salesperson. He worked at the same company for 25 years. Then he was **fired** from his job. He was **replaced** by a 27-year-old college graduate. Mr. Anderson's boss said he was **let go** because he looked too old.

Bill Barclay is a black doctor. He has enough money to buy an expensive house. Mr. Barclay has found a house in an all-white neighborhood. The **real estate agent** told him there are no houses for sale there. Mr. Barclay has seen at least two *For Sale* signs in that neighborhood.

Julio is a Mexican man. He has worked as a waiter for three years. He applies for a job as a waiter at an expensive restaurant. The manager tells Julio that there is a job in the kitchen washing dishes. He says there are no jobs for waiters. That afternoon, a U.S. college student with very little experience is **hired** as a waiter.

What Does It Mean?

New Word	Your Guess	Dictionary Definition
fired		
replaced		
let go		
real estate agent		
hired		

Discuss
The stories above are about different kinds of discrimination. What are they? What would you do in each situation?

Picture It

Think about what you have read. What are your ideas about discrimination? Write them on the tree below.

Certain kinds of information go in specific places on the tree:

1. On the roots, write what you think are the causes of discrimination.
2. On the trunk, write what you think is the definition of discrimination.
3. On the branches, write different types of discrimination.
4. On the leaves on the side of the tree, write examples of each type of discrimination.
5. On the leaves on the top of the tree, write some ways to solve the problem of discrimination.

Racial

Ignorance

Apply What You've Learned

Interview someone you know who comes from another country. This can be a classmate, neighbor, teacher, family member, friend, or co-worker.

Ask the person these questions, and write notes about their answers. Then, report to the class about the person you interviewed. Make sure you tell the class the person's name and how you know him or her.

Name of person interviewed: _____

1. Why did you come here?

_____

_____

2. What was your life like in your native country?

_____

_____

3. How has your life improved or not improved here?

_____

_____

4. Were you discriminated against in your native country? If so, how?

_____

_____

5. Have you been discriminated against in the U.S.? If so, how?

_____

_____

6. Do you want to stay here or go back to your native country? Why?

_____

_____

Write About You

Write about a time you experienced discrimination. What do you think caused the discrimination? How did you feel, and what did you do? If you think you never experienced discrimination, write about someone you know who did.

_____

_____

_____

_____

_____

_____

_____

_____

_____

_____

_____

_____

_____

_____

_____

_____

_____

_____

_____

_____

_____

Becoming an American

Assimilation means adapting
or fitting into a new country by
thinking and acting like its citizens.
Immigrants often want to become
part of a nation's culture. Have
you assimilated into U.S. culture?
Explain how.

Class in citizenship and English for
Italians, at the Hudson Park Library
on Seventh Avenue near Bleeker Street
(photograph by Marjory Collins for the Office of War
Information; collection of the Library of Congress)

Many immigrants come to the U.S. to make their dreams come true. Some may have difficulties along the way, but they never forget why they came here. Here are three of their stories.

Lisa Cheng came to the U.S. from Hong Kong. She felt she did not fit in when she first arrived. She wanted to look like other people in the U.S., and she was embarrassed about her accent. Finally, she learned to accept herself and to feel good about being Chinese. Now, Lisa works in a program helping other immigrants. She helps them learn how to deal with problems raising their children in the U.S. She knows how important children are to the future of this country. She also understands that she cannot change who she is. She knows immigrants should feel proud of their backgrounds.

Maxim Dolgi came here from Russia. He loved the easy-going attitude of people in the U.S. when he first arrived. It was very different from attitudes in his country. In Russia there was an excellent education system, but people were not friendly, like people are in the U.S. People in Russia were very formal. Maxim couldn't just go out on the street and talk to someone. Most of the time, he got together with friends in their homes. But they never talked about anything personal. It is very different for Maxim in the U.S. He feels that people here talk about things openly, and they have closer friendships. Maxim feels that education is important, but good friends are even more important.

Fernando Feria came here from Mexico when he was 24 years old. He had a good job in Mexico as a clerk in a textile factory. His brother was working in the U.S. and making a lot more money. Fernando decided to move here for better pay. At first, he worked 16 hours a day at two jobs. He was impressed by "the power of the dollar." In Mexico he had to save for months just to buy a pair of shoes. Here he could pay his expenses and still save money. Today Fernando manages a large apartment building in New York City and has started a small construction business. He feels that if people work hard in the U.S., they can get ahead.

Group of Jewish war orphans brought to America in 1921
(collection of the Ellis Island National Monument)

About the Story

1. Lisa had problems when she first came to the U.S. What were these, and how did she overcome them?

2. Why did Maxim find it easier to make friends in the U.S. than in Russia?

3. Fernando was impressed by "the power of the dollar." What did he mean by this?

4. Why does Lisa feel she has an important job?

5. What different things do Fernando and Maxim like about this country?

What's Your Experience?

How do the stories in this reading compare with your own experiences? What was your reason for coming to the U.S.? Did this country meet your expectations?

What Do You Think?

1. Lisa Cheng was embarrassed about her accent and about how she looked. How do you think being different affects immigrants' feelings about themselves in the U.S.?

2. Maxim Dolgi liked Americans' friendliness. Why do you think people acted so differently in his native country?

3. What qualities did Fernando need to succeed in the U.S.?

Words You Can Use: Immigration & Naturalization

As an immigrant, you may hear or need to use some of the words below:

asylum   permanent resident
citizenship   refugee
green card   visa
immunity   voter registration
naturalization

Try It Out

Write what you know about each of these words on the lines below. Use separate paper if necessary. Share this information with the class.

Example: **asylum:** This is the protection that a government gives someone who can prove he or she is being persecuted because of religion, race, political opinion, or nationality.

citizenship: _____

voter registration: _____

immunity: _____

green card: _____

permanent resident: _____

refugee: _____

visa: _____

naturalization: _____

Discuss

Do you know what laws correspond to each of these words? For example, do you know how to become a citizen or how to get a green card? Discuss what you know with the class.

How to Say It: Future Tense with *Will* and *Going to*

• We use *will* to talk about a future event or action.
  Example: In two years, I *will* become a citizen.

• We also use *will* to predict the future.
  Example: One day, I think all people *will* be free.

• *Going to* is used in less formal statements than *will*. We use *going to* when we talk about plans for the future. Use a form of *be* with *going to*.
  Example: I am *going to* visit my native country next summer.

• We also use *going to* for events we think will happen very soon.
  Example: I am *going to* get my citizenship next week.

Try It Out

A. Read again about Lisa, Maxim, and Fernando. Using the word *will*, predict what will happen to them in 10 years. Then make a prediction about yourself in 10 years.

Name	Prediction
Lisa Cheng:	_____
Maxim Dolgi:	_____
Fernando Feria:	_____
Me:	_____

B. Answer the following questions using *going to.* Write complete sentences. Share your answers with the class.

1. When are you *going to* finish your ESL classes?

_____

2. When are you *going to* visit your native country?

_____

3. When are you *going to* become a citizen?

_____

Put It Together

A. Predict when you or someone you know will be eligible for each of the following. Use the word *will*. Write your ideas below. Share your predictions with the class.

Example: citizenship: <u>I will get U.S. citizenship in five years.</u>

1. citizenship: _____

2. green card: _____

3. visa: _____

4. voter registration: _____

5. permanent resident: _____

B. Write the names of five people in the class. Predict what you think they will be doing in five years. Share your predictions with the class.

Name of person	**Prediction**
_____	_____
_____	_____
_____	_____
_____	_____
_____	_____

C. What activities do you have planned for next week? Write some things you are *going to* do. Share your plans with the class.

Example: I am *going to* have a party with my friends.

_____

_____

_____

_____

Ernesto Ibanez is an immigrant from El Salvador. His words are true for many of the immigrants who come to the U.S.

Some of the words in the reading are in bold. Try to guess the meanings of these new words. Then find the meanings in a dictionary.

The Immigration Experience

"It doesn't matter under what **circumstances** we got here. Many of us had the **privilege** to cross the U.S. border sitting down for a few hours in an airplane. Many others came here as refugees. Others came as students. Many had to leave their families, and they are here because their jobs are here, but their hearts are in their country. However, we all have something in common: We all want to **achieve** the American Dream. In other words, it is the same dream with the same **consequences**, and it is the same emotional **distress** that affects everyone. One has to force oneself to keep moving forward."

What Does It Mean?

New Word	Your Guess	Dictionary Definition
circumstance	_____	_____
privilege	_____	_____
achieve	_____	_____
consequences	_____	_____
distress	_____	_____

Discuss

Immigrants have been coming to the U.S. for over 200 years. What are some of the reasons immigrants come to this country today? What are their hopes and dreams?

Picture It

In the top box, write your dream for your life in the U.S. In the five boxes below that, list in order the most important steps you need to take to achieve this dream. Start with the first step at the bottom. Write the steps you will take after that, leading to your goal.

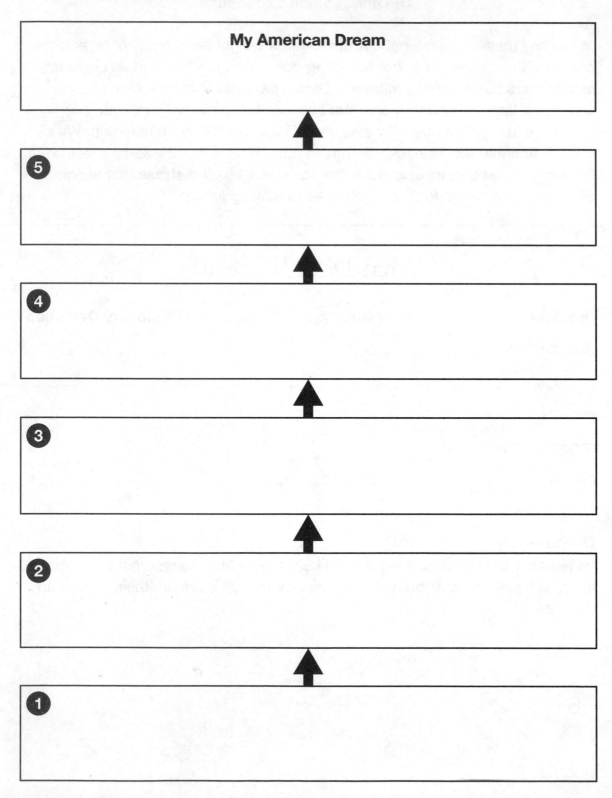

My American Dream

5

4

3

2

1

Apply What You've Learned

A. Write three goals that you have for your life. Talk to two or more students in your class. Get suggestions about how to achieve your goals. Write their advice on the lines below.

Goal 1: _____

_____

_____

_____

Goal 2: _____

_____

_____

_____

Goal 3: _____

_____

_____

_____

B. Here is a time line for completing goals. Select one of the goals that you wrote about above. Below the time line, write each step that you need to take in order to complete this goal. Use the advice your classmates gave you and your own ideas. Then, write each step on the time line with the date by which you hope to complete it. At the end of the time line, write the date for completing your goal.

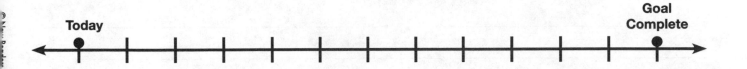

Write About You

What are your hopes and dreams for yourself and your family? What difficulties or problems do you think you will have to overcome? How do you think your life will be different 10 years from now?

_____

_____

_____

_____

_____

_____

_____

_____

_____

_____

_____

_____

_____

_____

_____

_____

_____

_____

_____

Resource
Lessons

Finding Information

There are several free resources from which you can get information. Three of these are available in any community. These are the library, the telephone book, and the Internet.

PUBLIC LIBRARIES

Public libraries in the U.S. are free and open to everyone. It is not necessary to be a U.S. citizen to get a library card. You need only a picture ID and proof of your address, such as a telephone or electric bill.

What You Can Find in the Public Library
- Library collections include not only books but also magazines, newspapers, academic journals, audio cassettes, CDs, DVDs, and videos.
- In most libraries, there are computers that the public can use, free of charge.
- There are many books you can check out, to take home and use for a period of time. These include fiction titles and a wide variety of nonfiction resources, covering everything from U.S. history to cookbooks.
- There are also reference materials that you can use in the library. These include encyclopedias, dictionaries, phone books, and reference books such as almanacs or government directories. These reference materials are available in print and/or electronically.
- Libraries also have books on tape. This is an excellent way to improve your English. With both the book and the tape, you can read the words and listen to them at the same time.
- Generally, libraries have separate sections of books for children and young adults. Many of the young adult titles are easier for English language learners to read. The catalog and the spine of the book usually have a **YA** to indicate this type of book.
- Most libraries also offer various interesting programs. Some libraries have storytelling for young children. Many libraries have free ESL and literacy programs, computer workshops, and job hunting workshops.

Activity:
Go to your local library. Find out what programs the library offers. Share this information with your classmates.

Name of library: _____

Programs: _____

_____

How to Find a Book in the Public Library

The library catalog lists what books are in the library and where to find them. Some libraries still have old fashioned card catalogs. The books are indexed on small cards. Today, however, most libraries use computer indexes or catalogs. To use a computerized catalog, read the instructions on the computer screen.

Catalogs arrange books alphabetically in three ways: by **title, author,** and **subject.** To find a book, look it up by its title, author, or general subject.

Title entries begin with the book's title. When a title begins with *An, A,* or *The,* the entry is found by looking under the first letter of the next word in the title. For example, *The Lost World* would be listed under *L; An Early Summer* would be listed under *E.*

Author entries are found under the author's last name. They are listed by last name, first name. For example, books by William Shakespeare would be found under *Shakespeare, William.*

Subject entries are based on the general topic of the book. Many books are listed under two or more subjects. For example, the book, *A History of Multicultural America: The Great Migrations,* might be found under these subjects: *American history, Immigration,* or *Multicultural.*

Activity:

Go to your local library or your school's library. Practice using the computerized catalog.

• Write the name of a book you would like to find: _____

• Type or click on a letter to start your search. Probably you can use these:
  T = title, **A** = Author, **S** = Subject (or Keyword).

• If you know the book's title, enter it.

• If you know the book's author, enter his or her name. Put the last name before the first name. (You may find that there are several books by the same author.)

• If you do not know the title or the author, enter the subject or a keyword.

• Did you find your book?

Finding a Book on the Shelves
The library has many different types of books:

Works of **fiction** present stories that an author makes up. They include novels and short stories. All fiction books are arranged in alphabetical order according to the last name of the author. Go to the fiction section of the library and look for the first three letters of the author's last name.

A **nonfiction** book contains facts about a subject. These books are arranged on the shelves by call numbers (see below). Each nonfiction book has a label giving the call number for that book. Call numbers are usually in the upper left-hand corner of each index card in a card catalog. They are also on the computer screen as part of a computerized catalog entry.

Biographies are true stories about real people, either alive or dead. They are grouped under the call number 921 and arranged on the shelves in alphabetical order by the last name of the person whom the biography is about. For example, *Edward R. Murrow,* by Anne Fordham, will be located under *Murrow* on the shelves.

Each main subject area has its own set of call numbers:
- 000-099 General Books
- 100-199 Philosophy
- 200-299 Religion
- 300-399 Social Sciences
- 400-499 Language
- 500-599 Pure Science
- 600-699 Technology
- 700-799 The Arts, Recreation
- 800-899 Literature
- 900-999 Geography and History

Activity:

Go to the library. Follow these steps to find the book *War and Peace in Central America* by Frank McNeil in a computerized catalog. For this activity, use the subject *Central American history* to find the book.

- Read the instructions on the screen.
- Type a letter to start your search. Since you are looking for a **subject,** type the letter *S* and press the return key.
- Type in a word or words about your subject and press the return key. Try *Central American history.* (You do not have to use capital letters for your search.)
- Look at the subjects that come up on your screen and choose the one that is closest to your subject. Type or click on the number next to the subject you want.
- Read the titles and locations. Choose the book you want.
- Look for the call number. Write it down. Then find the book on the shelves.

Activity:

Find a book about life in the tenements on New York City's Lower East Side.

- Type in your subject.
- Look at the subjects that come up and pick a narrower subject if necessary.
- What books did you find?
- Choose two books and find them on the shelf.

Activity:

Find the books on tape in your library. Use the diagram that gives a map of the library, or ask a librarian.

- Choose a tape for a book that looks interesting to you. Some books on tape are abridged, or shortened. Find a tape that has a recording of the complete book.
- If it is fiction, find the book on the shelves by using the author's last name.
- If it is nonfiction, find the call number for the book in the catalog.
- Listen to the tape while you read the book.

The phone book does not contain cell phone numbers.

TELEPHONE BOOKS

Telephone books provide the names and numbers of people and businesses in your city. Most phone books also have listings for government offices, schools, hospitals, and other important institutions. Many also have information about the community.

The White Pages

The White Pages lists telephone numbers for people and businesses. People's names are listed in alphabetical order by their last names. Businesses are usually listed in a separate section. They are in alphabetical order by the first important word in the name of the business. In some locations, people and businesses are listed together in alphabetical order.

Many phone books have special listings for government offices. Generally, there are separate sections listing government offices for the city and/or county, the state, and the U.S. federal government. For example, the post office is under the *Federal* heading.

The first page of the White Pages often lists emergency numbers. Some books also list area codes for every major city and provide a map of area codes in the country. International calling codes, community service numbers, and ZIP Code information can also be found in some White Pages.

Activity:

Look up the following places in your phone book. Write the information on the lines below. In which section did you find it?

- Phone number and address of a museum _____
- Phone number of the Poison Control Center _____
- Phone number of the Fire Department _____
- Phone number of the Police Department _____
- Phone number and address of a school in your area _____
- Phone number and address of a person you know _____

The Yellow Pages

The Yellow Pages has names, addresses, and telephone numbers for companies, institutions, organizations, and businesses in your city. Unlike the listings in the White Pages, these are listed in the Yellow Pages by category, and then in alphabetical order within the category. For example, *Joe's Hardware Store* is listed under the category heading *Hardware*. There is often a heading index in the back of the book. Some Yellow Pages include emergency and community information, as well as government listings.

Activity:

Use the Yellow Pages. Look for the following places. Answer the questions with the information that you find.

1. What are the names of two stores that sell **mattresses**?

_____

2. Look up the name of a **language school** that teaches English? What is the name, phone number, and address?

_____

3. Look up the name of a school that trains you to be a **beautician**. (You might find this information under **beauty** or **schools**.)

_____

4. Look up the name of a Chinese restaurant in your city. Try to find a restaurant near your home. What is the name, address, and phone number? (You should find this information under **restaurants**.)

_____

Activity:

Look in the front of your Yellow Pages. Does your phone book give any instructions about what to do in case of an emergency? If so, what emergencies does it cover? What advice does it give?

_____

_____

_____

_____

THE INTERNET

The Internet is a speedy tool for finding information about almost any subject. You can use the Internet on your own computer or on a school or public library computer. These public computers are normally free of charge. Many public libraries and community centers also offer programs where you can learn about using computers and the Internet. Library programs are usually free of charge.

You use a computer program called a search engine to look for information on the Internet. When you use a search engine, you type in a keyword to look for information, just as you do when you look for a book with a subject index on the library catalog. For example, if you type in the word *immigration,* you will find every site that has the word *immigration* in it. There could be thousands of entries. You should be as specific as you can to narrow your search. For example, *Chinese immigration* has fewer entries than *immigration. Chinese immigration + New York* has even fewer categories. Click on the site you want to go to. If you know the exact address of the *web site,* you can go directly there without searching through numerous sites.

Internet Language

Here are a few words you might use when working on the Internet.

WWW (World Wide Web)—technology that lets you get information on the Internet

Web site—a page or group of pages on the World Wide Web

E-mail—short term for *electronic mail*

Online—to be connected to a computer or computer network

Log on/Sign on—to connect to a computer system, usually with a password

Address Bar—the space where you type in a web address.

Browser—a computer program that lets you find and use web sites and information on the Internet

Activity:

On a computer, type in each of the following addresses. Look through the information on the web site. Write three interesting facts you find at each web site.

The addresses for web sites often change. Sometimes a site becomes unavailable. The addresses below are as up-to-date as possible, but they may change.

www.tenement.org At this site, you can take a tour through the Tenement Museum even if you don't live in New York City. You can also read more about some of the immigrants from 97 Orchard Street who are featured in this book.

_____

_____

_____

http://uscis.gov/graphics/citizenship/welcomeguide/index.htm This site contains practical information to help immigrants in their daily lives in the U.S.

_____

_____

_____

http://www.onlinenewspapers.com Here you can read online newspapers from all over the world, even from your native country or the city or town where you live now.

_____

_____

_____

http://www.mapquest.com On this web site you can find directions for going from one place to another place in your city or directions for driving between any two points in the world.

_____

_____

_____

MY OWN INFORMATION GUIDE

Talking to other people is a good way to get information that you need or share information that you have. This is also called **networking**. For example, you may know a great place to learn about computers, or you may want to get the e-mail address and phone number of a friend.

In the boxes below, write addresses, phone numbers, web sites, book titles, or other useful information to share with your classmates. Make sure you put the information in the right box so you can easily find it. You may want to include questions about information you want or need. See if your classmates can give you that information.

Immigration	**Friends and Family**

Health	**Shopping**

Schools and Training Programs

Restaurants

Employment

English Language

More Information

Getting a Job

Getting a job today is different from the way it was 100 years ago. Computers, fax machines, and phones have changed the way people look for jobs. But no matter how you look for a job, you will need to know the following:

- What skills you have and what skills you need for a job
- How to write a resume
- How to fill out a job application
- How to interview for a job

SKILLS

When you think about getting a job, you must identify what skills you have and what skills you need for a certain job.

Activity:
Here are five different jobs. Write two skills that a person needs for each job.

Example:
Teacher:

Speaks clearly
_____

Works well with children
_____

Nurse:

_____

_____

Computer Programmer:

_____

_____

Construction Worker:

_____

_____

Salesperson:

_____

_____

Activity:

List three jobs you or someone you know had in your native country. What skills were needed for each one?

Job: _____

Skills: _____

_____

Job: _____

Skills: _____

_____

Job: _____

Skills: _____

_____

Activity:

Write two jobs that you would like to have in this country. List skills that are needed for each one.

Check (✓) the skills you already have.

Put a star (✱) next to the skills you need to get.

Job #1: _____

Skills Needed:

_____

_____

_____

Job #2: _____

Skills Needed:

_____

_____

_____

WRITING A RESUME

A resume is a summary of your work experience, education, and skills. When you are looking for a job, an employer may ask for your resume. Here are the main parts of a resume.

- **Personal data**: Name, address, telephone number, fax number (if available), and e-mail address

- **Goal**: The job or type of job you want

- **Education**: A list of schools you attended, the dates, and the degrees (or certificates) you received from each school. List the most recent school first. Mention any honors or awards you received.

- **Work experience**: A list of all jobs you have had in your native country and in the U.S., including a brief description of your duties and your dates of employment. List your most recent job first. Mention any awards you received and any special accomplishments or contributions you made.

- **Special skills**: A list of languages that you speak and any business skills you possess, such as computer or typing skills

- **References**: The names and phone numbers or e-mail addresses of teachers and/or former employers who will give you a recommendation. Usually, you do not write these names on your resume. Instead, you write *References available upon request.* This means that if the employer wants a reference, you will give him or her the names of people who know you and can describe how you work.

A resume gives an employer a first impression of who you are. It's important that your spelling and grammar are perfect. Have a teacher or a friend who speaks fluent English check your resume before you send it to an employer.

Sample Resume

There are many different ways to write a resume. Here is one sample.

Yolanda Rivera
58 Allen Street
New York, NY 10002
212-555-2121
Yolanda@hotmail.com

Goal

Part-time or full-time sales work in an office

Education

1996-2000   New York Business College, New York, NY
B.A. in Computers.
Also studied business administration.

1992-1996   John Adams High School, Brooklyn, NY

Work Experience

2000–present   Ajax Electronics Store. Work as a sales clerk in Computer
Department. Also handle phone and cash register.
Received *Employee of the Month* twice in each of last
two years.

1998–2000   Tracy's Department Store. Worked part-time as a file clerk
in the Accounting Department. Responsibilities included
sending out bills and collecting payments.

Special Skills

Fluent in Spanish
Can type 50 words per minute
Can use PC and Macintosh computers

References

Available upon request

My Resume Worksheet

Before putting together a resume, it's useful to first write down your personal information on a worksheet. This worksheet will help you organize the information so you know what to include on the resume.

Activity:

Fill in the following information. Use a separate sheet of paper if necessary.

Often you need to send a cover letter with your resume. This is a short letter that introduces you to the employer. Be sure to state which job you are applying for and why you think you would be good at the job. Say that you are enclosing your resume.

Name: _____

Address: _____

Phone: _____ **E-Mail:** _____

Job Goal (the kind of work you want to do):

_____

Education

Any post-college education or training program: _____

College: _____

Any trade school or job training: _____

High School: _____

Work Experience (Include what you did at each job)

Most recent job: _____

_____

Previous jobs: _____

_____

_____

Special Skills and Languages (languages you speak, computer, or other skills you have):

_____

_____

THE JOB APPLICATION

When you apply for a job, you will be asked to fill out a job application. It requires a lot of the same information that you put on your resume.

Activity:

This worksheet asks for some of the information that you will need to fill out an application. Complete the worksheet with your information.

> **You may find it useful to copy these two pages and take the copy with you when you are looking for a job. Then you will have the information handy to fill out applications.**

Personal Information

Social Security number: _____

Address/Phone number/E-mail: _____

Immigration status (Citizenship? Visa? Green Card?): _____

A-number (if applicable): _____

Employment Information

Position desired: _____

Name of current employer: _____

Current position/responsibilities: _____

When you can start working: _____

Hours you can work: _____

How you heard about the job: _____

Education/City (Country)/Dates

High school: _____

College/University: _____

Trade or Business school: _____

Job training program(s) _____

General

Special skills: _____

_____

Special activities or hobbies: _____

U.S. Military service: _____

Former Employers/City (Country)/Position/Dates of Employment:

_____

_____

_____

_____

_____

_____

References (Names and addresses or phone numbers of people who are not related to you, but know you well):

_____

_____

_____

Tips for Filling out a Job Application

1. Make sure you read all the directions carefully before you begin to write on the application form.

2. Print all information clearly. Carefully print on the lines.

3. Use blue or black ink. Use pencil only if you are specifically asked to do that.

4. Bring your resume and the names and telephone numbers of your references with you. Make sure you also have your Social Security number, visa, or citizenship status with you.

5. Use your job application information sheet (from pages 123 - 124) to be sure your information is accurate and complete.

6. When you list your education and jobs, give the most recent ones first.

7. You do not have to reveal your religion, age, race, or marital status.

8. Bring a dictionary with you to look up any words you do not understand.

9. Sign only on the line where your signature is required.

10. Don't be afraid to ask any questions that you have.

THE INTERVIEW

The interview is a meeting between you and an employer. It gives the employer an opportunity to find out more about you. It also gives you a chance to find out more about the job and the company. Here are some tips for a good interview.

Before the Interview

1. Practice talking with a friend or classmate about yourself. This is a great preparation for the real interview.
2. Learn all you can about the job and the company, including salary and benefits.
3. Prepare two or three questions about the job and the company, to show your interest.
4. Practice answering possible interview questions. Here are some questions an employer might ask you:
    - Tell me about yourself.
    - Why do you think you would like this particular job?
    - What kind of work experience have you had?
    - What can you contribute to this company?
    - What would you like to be doing five years from now? Ten years from now? What are your long-range goals?
    - Why did you leave your last job?
    - Do you prefer working by yourself or with others?
    - What are your strengths and weaknesses?
    - Why do you think we should hire you?
    - What salary do you want?
5. Bring your resume.
6. Bring a copy of your diploma or any other degree from your native country. Have it translated.
7. Arrive at least 15 minutes early. This will give you the opportunity to relax, check your appearance, and look through any literature about the company.
8. Be neat and clean. Do not wear clothes or jewelry that attract attention. Shirts should not be unbuttoned more than one button. Women should not wear tight, sexy clothing.
9. Prepare questions to ask the interviewer about job responsibilities.

During The Interview

Here are some tips from people who have been interviewed about what to do and what not to do during a job interview.

Do

1. Begin the interview with a firm handshake, a self-introduction, and a smile.
2. Speak clearly and look directly at the interviewer.
3. Tell your interviewer what your skills are and what you can do for the company.
4. Give honest answers to all questions. If you don't know an answer, tell the interviewer you will get back to him or her. Then do it.
5. Ask questions about the job. This not only shows interest; it also lets you know if this is the job for you. Here are some sample questions:
   • Whom would I be working with? Whom would I be working for?
   • What would my responsibilities be?
   • What skills are important for the job?
6. If you are not offered the job during the interview, ask when you may call to find out about the job. If the interviewer tells you that the job is not for you, ask that person if there are other employers you could contact for a job.
7. Be sure you get a business card with the person's name and phone number. Make sure you say *thank you* at the end of the interview.

Don't

1. Do not smoke, drink, or chew gum during the interview.
2. Do not say anything negative about your past or present job.
3. Do not discuss personal or financial problems.
4. Do not ask the interviewer any personal questions.

After the Interview

After you have an interview, write a short note thanking the person who interviewed you for his or her time. This is another chance to express your interest in working at the company. Even if you are not offered the job, this is a good way to **network**. **Networking** means making contacts for future opportunities. Another job may even come up at the same company at another time. A *thank you* note helps an employer remember who you are.

Activity:

Do a practice interview with a partner for a job of your choice.
One of you will act as the employer, asking questions about the applicant. One of you will be applying for the job. After your practice interview, make a list of things you think you did well and a list of things you want to improve for a real interview. Ask your partner for suggestions. Write on the chart below.

Things I Did Well	Things I Need to Improve
I spoke clearly.	I must learn more about the company.